no-churn ice cream

no-churn
ice cream

~~~~~~~

over 100 simply delicious
no-machine frozen treats

LESLIE BILDERBACK

Photographs by Teri Lyn Fisher

ST. MARTIN'S GRIFFIN

New York

acknowledgments

Thanks to BJ Berti at St. Martin's Press, for her continued support; to Katherine Latshaw for her brilliant ideas; to the staff and customers at Heirloom Bakery for being my flavor guinea pigs; to Dr. Manuel Aguilar for his patience; and especially to Emma, Claire, and Bill for their support, exquisite taste buds, and willingness to give up so much freezer space for ice cream. Your sacrifice is not forgotten

www.stmartins.com

The Library of Congress Cataloging-in-Publication Data is available upon request.

ISBN 978-1-250-05438-8 (trade paperback)
ISBN 978-1-4668-7766-5 (e-book)

St. Martin's Griffin books may be purchased for educational, business, or promotional use. For information on bulk purchases, please contact the Macmillan Corporate and Premium Sales Department at 1-800-221-7945, extension 5442, or write to specialmarkets@macmillan.com.

Book design by Jennifer Daddio / Bookmark Design & Media Inc.
Editor: BJ Berti
Assistant Editor: Courtney Littler
Production Manager: Adriana Coada

First Edition: May 2015

10 9 8 7 6 5 4 3 2 1

To all the international servicemen and women, doctors, dentists, veterinarians, and myriad specialists who welcomed me aboard the USS *Pearl Harbor* for the Pacific Partnership Humanitarian Mission of 2013—and especially the CSs and FSAs who kept them fed (the only crew making croissants from scratch in the middle of the Pacific Ocean). I started this book on board, and finished it with y'all in mind.

contents

Vanilla Ice Cream Sprinkle Pops

introduction

~~~

Welcome, extreme ice cream lovers. You clearly are a breed apart if you are willing to make ice cream yourself. Congratulations on finding not only this quick-and-easy ice cream method—without an ice cream machine—but dozens and dozens of easy, impressive, satisfying dessert ideas. Here you will learn about flavor compatibility, plate presentations, food history, and nifty tricks of the trade.

Sure, sometimes it is enough to just buy something at the store ready-made—something we all do from time to time. There is no shame in that. But there are times when it is not enough to simply provide a dessert. If you are truly interested in food as a means of expressing love, appreciation, and art, then you will enjoy the following pages. Yes, it is darn easy. Crazy easy. But it is also so good that no one needs to ever know just how easy it was.

If you are interested in dessert, flavor, and creativity, you are in the right place.

ICE CREAM BASICS

This no-churn ice cream method is based on the classic French dessert called *parfait*. Unlike the American layered parfait your grandma made with Jell-O and Cool Whip, the French version is vanilla custard, lightened with whipped cream, and frozen in a loaf pan. Once frozen, the French parfait is sliced, like a frozen sweet pâté.

While this no-churn ice cream method nods to the classic, it is 100 percent built to scoop. It is also built to make in a hurry, with no ice cream machine, and no difficult techniques (unless you want them). This is accomplished in two ways: First, the air normally incorporated by a churning ice cream machine is added instead in the form of whipped cream. Second, the custard, which is a classic pastry preparation that takes some time to master, is replaced by sweetened condensed milk. If you are interested in learning the recipe for custard, it is here, too, in the final chapter.

The intention is not only to get you to make ice cream at home, but to get you to make really good ice cream at home, repeatedly. Toward that goal, you will find both classic and cutting edge–flavored recipes in this book.

You will also find myriad accompaniments, because the enjoyment of a dessert comes not only from the way it tastes, but also the things it is paired with and the way it is presented. Each recipe offers accompaniment ideas. And because I know you are going to get excited about the possibilities, there is a section to help you with the basics of dessert creation.

Start simple, by all means. But don't stop there.

A LITTLE HISTORY OF ICE CREAM

There are a dozen stories about the inception of ice cream. Few are probably true, and even fewer are actually discussing ice cream. Most are really about early snow cones. For instance, it is a common tale that Nero had snow brought into Rome from the mountains by human chain so he could sweeten it with honey and wine. Not ice cream, but at least it sounds fairly palatable. Even earlier during the T'ang dynasty, around 3000 BC, Imperial treats of shaved ice dripping with fermented mare's milk and camphor were created. (No, really.) This was not really ice cream either, but at least we were adding dairy to the list of ingredients (of a sort). If it is true that Marco Polo brought these treats back to Europe, I find it hard to believe that he would have been taken seriously, especially at the suggestion that Venetians start milking their horses.

While the Italians love to tout the ever-present importance of Catherine de Medici on the history of food (which is, as far as I can tell, wildly exaggerated) it was, in all likelihood, the Italians (probably Sicilians) who first gave us frozen custard, which has come to be known in that region as *gelato*. It probably did spread to France (though probably not with the Medicis), and followed the French aristocracy to the far reaches of the world, including the new one, with my favorite food-loving president, Thomas Jefferson.

Lots of recipes for ice cream pop up in early American cookbooks, but the majority of early recipes are simply infused cream, sweetened and flavored primarily with fruits, then placed in a larger container of ice and salt and stirred. Cooling down the sweet cream (the richest part of the milk) with ice thickened it. The earliest written recipe for vanilla bean custard–based ice cream was probably brought from France to the United States in the 1780s, but it is unlikely that it was the first recipe of its kind, as the written recipe always follows its widespread use.

THE INGREDIENTS

CREAM

There are many creams on the market, which can make shopping for these recipes confusing. Rest at ease, America—they will all work in these recipes. Different versions of cream contain different fat contents. That means, when you want it richer, you need to increase the fat content in your cream, and vice versa. Professional pastry chefs use manufacturing cream, with a whopping 40% butterfat. Regular grocery store whipping cream has 30%, while heavy cream (sometimes called heavy whipping cream) has 36%. The benefit of the added fat (besides allowing you to buy larger clothes) is that heavier cream holds its peak longer. This is important if you intend on holding whipped cream for a number of hours (as bakeries do in display cases), but for the average home cook, it isn't an issue.

MILK

There is a lot of talk about milk these days, not much of it good, and most of it revolves around avoiding it completely. That's all well and good, but really, I love milk, and while it is replaceable (almond milk and soy milk work perfectly well in all recipes in this book as substitutes), in my opinion nothing is as good. I am all for saving the environment and being nice to cows—I really like cows. For that reason, I use organic milk from well-treated cows, although it costs more, because I would rather pay the extra bucks than think about cows in a factory farm. I also use almost exclusively fat-free milk, in my glass and in my recipes. This is a habit that I can't kick—whole milk just tastes too rich for me. But as with the cream, any milk you have will work fine. Experiments with richer or lighter milk will alter your results only slightly.

EGGS

Traditional ice cream is an egg custard. The recipes in this book are, for the most part, egg-free. Instead, the custard has been replaced with sweetened condensed milk. However, there are still a few egg recipes in these pages, so a little egg knowledge won't hurt. I will encourage you to buy cage-free eggs as much as possible, to prevent sad chickens. Use organic if you can. Most recipes in this book, and in every other one, assume you are using large eggs. Using medium or jumbo eggs won't harm a recipe much, especially if it calls for only one egg. The need to stick to large eggs is really only an issue when you begin to multiply a recipe by 10 or 20, or if you are baking for money. Paying customers tend to expect a product that is the same every time. In these cases, sticking to the large egg indicated is crucial. But, again, this is much less of an issue for home cooks.

For your information, a large egg white weighs 1 ounce, and a yolk weighs two-thirds of an ounce. This book rarely calls for ingredients by weight, but I think it's useful information to have.

Here's another egg fact: cooks in the United States are the only ones who store eggs in the refrigerator. In fact we have a weird and paranoid tendency to refrigerate lots of things un-necessarily. (How many of you have your ketchup in the fridge?) But eggs are less of a threat than you have been led to believe. It is salmonella that most cooks fear, but more cases of that disease have been transmitted via the skin of melons than eggs. And if it does come from an egg, chances are that it will be on the egg shell, something that is easily washable, and won't be affected by refrigeration. Storing eggs at room temperature benefits the baker. Chilled protein and fat are thicker, but eggs blend into recipes more easily and whites whip up higher when they are thinner. If you can muster the courage, consider keeping your eggs at room temperature. At the very least, leave them out for a few hours before you bake.

SUGAR AND SWEETENERS

Most recipes in this book call for granulated sugar, and in most recipes of the world granulated sugar is the default sugar. In other words, if the type of sugar is not specified in a recipe, it means granulated. Sugar comes from two sources: sugar cane and sugar beets. Either is fine, and their outcome is identical.

With little exception, granulated sugar can be substituted for by any number of other sweet-eners. Brown sugar can be substituted cup for cup. It is what comes naturally when sugar cane is boiled and the water reduced. The brown is molasses, which is extracted to create white sugar. In centuries past the extraction of molasses was done in varying degrees to create light or dark brown sugar, the dark having more molasses flavor. Today, however, it is cheaper for the large manufacturers to remove all the molasses, then stir it back in to create the brown versions. Sugar in the Raw, also known as turbinado sugar, is a coarser brown sugar. It takes a bit of heat to dissolve, so I usually reserve this for the top of pastries, where its pretty crystals will show. Sugar in the Raw is also my exclusive sugar for bruléed desserts. Its thickness and molasses content give it a higher flash point, meaning it takes longer for it to burn—a benefit when you are caramelizing with a torch.

Powdered sugar is nothing but pulverized white sugar. It comes in several grinds, designated by "x's" that indicate the number of times the sugar has been ground. The powdered sugar available in most grocery stores is 10x. Powdered sugar, confectioner's sugar, icing sugar, sucre glace, and 10x are all the same thing. In the United States this product has either cornstarch or wheat flour added to reduce clumping. This will not affect your recipes, but it may affect anyone with wheat allergies. Check the label.

Baker's sugar, or superfine sugar, is a grind somewhere between granulated and powdered. In my opinion, in most applications it is unnecessary. It has been misrepresented as the sugar professional chefs use, which is a brilliant marketing ploy, but also a lie. Superfine sugar is sometimes used by chefs in meringues or meringue-based recipes, but it is not necessary, and it is, in most cases, an extravagant expense few food service establishments can afford. There are few recipes I feel warrant superfine sugar, and for those, I simply grind my own by pulverizing granulated sugar a little more in the food processor. Ha! Take that, Mad Men.

Honey is a perfect substitute for sugar. It has a slightly acidic, floral aftertaste that lends itself well to a variety of fruits, wines, spices, and nuts. Most books refer to honey as being twice as sweet as sugar, but I have not found this to be a universal truth. I will, more often than not, add a nearly equal amount. The key is to know your honey, and taste your recipe as it is being made. Because honey is a natural product that relies on the nectar of random flowers, the level of sweetness varies greatly. The sweetness of mass-produced honey will be adjusted to maintain consistency, but this is not true of independent producers, and brand-to-brand sugar levels are not consistent.

Agave is another natural sweetener that can easily be used in place of sugar. Made from the same cactus plant as tequila, it has a hint of that flavor. (Of course technically, it is the tequila that has a hint of the agave flavor.) Agave has surged in popularity because it has been touted with a lower glycemic index than sugar, meaning it won't spike your blood sugar, which is a bonus for diabetics. Do not, however, think for a minute that agave is an artificial sugar. It is as natural as a sugar gets.

Stevia, also called sweet leaf or sugar leaf, has recently become widely available. It is a natural product extracted from the leaf of an herb, and it is three hundred times sweeter than sugar. It is popular because it also has a glycemic index of zero. It is super strong, so go easy, and use only a pinch.

Artificial sweeteners (aka non-nutritive sweeteners) will also work in these recipes, but please be aware of what you are eating. Most artificial sweeteners are chemically created, and there has been relatively little testing of the long-term effects of consumption.

SALT

Salt is the magical mineral that enhances flavor, which is why salt is an ingredient in nearly every recipe of this book. In most cases it is not intended to add saltiness. Just a pinch brings out the natural flavors of the dish. Left out, the recipes will seem bland.

Any salt will do, but these recipes call for kosher salt. I prefer this salt because it has the most neutral flavor. Other salts taste too much of chemicals, metal, or the sea. Kosher is purer, which is why many chefs use it, and not, as has been widely reported, because it is easily pinchable.

Of course, a cook's salt is a personal preference, and you can use any salt you choose in these recipes. There are several types of edible salt commonly available. Table salt is usually iodized. Potassium iodide is added as a dietary supplement to prevent iodine deficiency, a major cause of goiter and cretinism. Most table salt has a water-absorbing additive to keep it from clumping, and some manufacturers add fluoride as well.

Fleur de sel, literally translated as "salt flower," is natural sea salt, hand harvested and gourmet priced. It usually comes from specific locations, most notably off the coast of Brittany, in France. Each location produces distinct flavors due to the area's naturally occurring marine vegetation and minerals. Sea salt removed from the top layer of water is pale and delicate in flavor, while gray sea salt (*sel gris*), is allowed to sink and mix with the ocean water, giving it a more robust flavor. You will also find black salt, gray salt, pink salt, smoked salt, marsh salt, and even moon salt (harvested at night, not from the moon). You can spend quite a lot of money on salt, but beware: once it's mixed into foods, the unique character of these specialty salts is easily lost. Save them for sprinkling on foods that will benefit from their unique qualities. Salts are harvested throughout the world, and they make fun souvenirs of your travels. If you don't get out much, pricey salt can be easily found on the Internet.

SWEETENED CONDENSED MILK

This ingredient is the unsung hero of the pastry world. Invented in the United States by Gail Borden in the 1850s in response to the death of children due to bad milk, it made use of the Shaker vacuum pan as a method of reducing the water out of milk without curdling it. This enabled the milk to be canned more economically. Though it is possible to get unsweetened condensed milk, it is hard to find, as sugar helps prolong condensed milk's shelf life. Borden's contribution was, more than anything, the exacting sanitation standards he put his dairymen through. As a consequence of these standards, which included extra clean udders, routinely swept barn floors, and sanitized equipment, Borden's "Eagle Brand" milk has been a best-seller since the 1860s, and a champion of bake sales even today.

Evaporated milk is a similar, unsweetened product. But because it is substantially thinner, it is not recommended as a substitute for sweetened condensed milk in these recipes. It is used, however, in the gelato chapter to enrich the ice cream bases.

As stated earlier, sweetened condensed milk is used as a replacement for the classic ice cream custard, crème anglaise. If you are up for a challenge, that recipe appears on page 137 in the final chapter.

THE TECHNIQUES

WHIPPING

There is quite a lot of whipping in this book, so the technique bears mention. Whipping should be done with a whisk, either handheld or electric. The electric versions are, of course, faster, though whipping by hand is oddly satisfying.

The easiest way to whip is with a stand electric mixer. Handheld electric mixers are the second choice, and your last resort would be to beat by hand using a large bowl and a huge balloon whisk. Whipping by hand takes longer, and requires physical stamina, however, it is by far the coolest, most hard-core method. When I was in culinary school my instructor used to make us whip-race. The fastest whipper in the class got extra grade points, and was then pitted against the electric mixer for a grand prize (which I do not remember, because I washed out in the early rounds). I still whip by hand fairly frequently. Sometimes, especially with small amounts of egg or cream, the quantity to be whipped is too small to reach the whip of the electric mixer anyway. Also, sometimes I am just too lazy to pull out the machine.

Whipping requires that you capture air and bring it into the cream or eggs. The whisk is a perfect tool for this job. It has many wires in a cage shape that agitate the surface of the liquid, drawing in air. This works most efficiently when the whisk is drawn completely out of the liquid with each pass. Stirring in a slow circular motion does very little. You must use a circular scooping motion, as if you were grabbing the air with each pass. This takes more effort, but the end result comes quicker.

There are many different whisks available. Some have hard wires, but for whipping in air you want a soft-wired whisk. The softer wires move back and forth with each stroke, adding more air, and speeding the task. Firm wire whisks are good for mixing thicker things, like pâte à choux or mashed potatoes. If money is no object, the classic balloon whisk, with the exaggerated bulb shape, makes the fastest work of whisking. The balloon whisk, however, is good for little else. So if you are more frugal, buy a large regular (non-balloon) whisk with the softest wires you can find, which will serve you in many other purposes.

The stand mixer is the preferred electric mixer of professionals, and usually comes with several attachments, including a whisk, a paddle, and a hook. A handheld electric beater is what my mom and grandmother had. These whisks (usually referred to as beaters) will do the trick, but because the wires are fatter and there is less space between them, the whipping in of air takes longer. Work the beaters on the surface of the liquid as much as possible (without spattering the walls) to make a lot of bubbles, which will incorporate as much air as possible.

FOLDING

Few mixing techniques are as nerve-wracking as folding, probably because pastry chefs have scared you into fearing it. Yes, overfolding can deflate a recipe. But it's not like it will cause toxicity, or an international incident. You might have to start over, but big whoop.

The purpose of folding is to incorporate two ingredients, one of which is usually full of air. To do this, and to maintain all that air, the fewer the strokes the better. Folding is commonly done with a rubber spatula, but I have found that more efficient folding can be done with a whisk. Instead of the rubber spatula's single blade passing through the mix, a whisk passes twenty to forty wires through a mixture with each stroke, which accomplishes the job in far fewer passes and, therefore, with less chance of deflation. For this purpose, as with whisking, a soft wire whisk is preferable.

FREEZING

Clearly the recipes in this book require that you have a freezer. If you don't, either put the book down right now, or go make friends with your neighbor with the freezer. Tiny freezers, like those in some mini refrigerators (I'm talking to you, college students) are not always adequate. Some "chillers" do not dip to the 0 to 5°F necessary to freeze your ice cream mixtures. Other things that might hinder the freeze are excessively cluttered freezers (a good excuse to clean it out, perhaps) and those in desperate need of defrosting. (That iceberg lining the walls of your freezer is hogging all the cold air.)

The container you choose to freeze your ice cream in is less important than all the other equipment. Just be sure your container will actually fit in your freezer first. I have used everything from metal loaf pans to recycled sour cream tubs. Glass is not impossible to use, provided you are careful about bringing it up to room temperature. Too fast a temperature increase will cause cracking in most glass. Lids are not necessary, unless you intend long-term freezing. These recipes call for you to press plastic wrap or waxed paper directly on the surface of the ice cream base for the freezer. This prevents a layer of ice crystals and frost from forming on the surface. A lid will help keep out odors from extended freezer stays.

One final tidbit of information to keep in mind—a thin layer of ice cream will freeze faster than a thick one. That means if you are in an über-rush, use something with a wide surface area, like a brownie pan. You are welcome!

the classics

T o begin your no-churn adventure, it makes sense to start with the basics. The recipes in this chapter are standards that you will easily find already made in your market freezer. But if your goal is to create your own unique flavors, it is necessary to understand the simple bases. These flavors, boring as they are, are crucial tools in the art of dessert making. They are the blank canvas on which far more interesting plates can be created. Understand these first—then let your creative juices flow.

vanilla ice cream

MAKES ABOUT 1 QUART OF ICE CREAM

Here it is. The one from which all others were born. The Holy Grail of ice cream flavors, and the best way for you to begin your no-churn experiments.

INGREDIENTS

One 13-ounce can sweetened condensed milk

1 cup milk

½ vanilla bean, scraped

1 teaspoon pure vanilla extract

Pinch of salt

1 tablespoon fresh lemon juice

2 cups heavy cream

METHOD

1. In a large bowl, combine the sweetened condensed milk, milk, vanilla bean, vanilla extract, salt, and lemon juice.

2. In a separate bowl, whip the heavy cream until it reaches soft peak. Fold the cream gently into the milk mixture, then transfer to a shallow freezable container.

3. Cover with plastic wrap or waxed paper pressed directly on the surface of the ice cream, and place in the freezer for 6 hours.

4. Scoop and serve the finished ice cream with fresh berries, chocolate or caramel sauce, or a drizzle of Kahlúa.

VARIATIONS

VANILLA, LEMON, AND ANISE: This flavor combination is common in the Basque region of Spain and France, and although it is amazing on its own, it also serves as a great platform for fruity flavors. Add to the milk mixture the finely grated zest of 1 lemon, ½ teaspoon of toasted and finely ground anise seeds (toast in a dry skillet and grind in a coffee mill). Fennel seeds will also work, as will a teaspoon of Pernod or Sambuca. Be wary of anise extract—it can be too strong for this subtle blend.

VANILLA-CARDAMOM: This is the perfect blend of sweet, spicy, and floral flavors. Gently warm the cup of milk in the microwave or on the stovetop, then add 1 teaspoon of crushed cardamom pods. Set it aside to steep and cool completely. Drain off the spice, and proceed with the recipe as directed.

Strawberry, Vanilla-Lobster, and
Vanilla-Tomato Ice Creams

VANILLA

There is nothing plain about vanilla. As far as I am concerned, it is a miracle flavor. Floral, spicy, exotic, and rich, it can work alone or in conjunction with dozens of other flavors.

The acquisition of this flavor is as amazing as the way it feels in your mouth. Vanilla comes from the pod of the orchid *Vanilla planifolia*. The Spanish found it being used in the New World, and brought it to Europe, where they failed miserably at its cultivation because, as they soon discovered, V. *planifolia* can only be pollinated by Mexican bees and hummingbirds. Artificial pollination was tried and failed. But where there's a will, there's a way, and the cunning French shipped orchids to the island of Bourbon (known today as Réunion) and figured out a fast way to hand-pollinate (forever guaranteeing vanilla's high price). By the turn of the twentieth century Bourbon and the neighboring Madagascar produced nearly all of the world's vanilla.

Today we have three vanilla bean varieties on the market: Madagascar beans are used mainly for extract production; Tahitian beans are more aromatic than flavorful, and as a result are used more often for perfumes than pastries; and Mexican beans are fat, fragrant, and flavorful. The extract from Mexico is my personal favorite, but it can be hard to find. Whichever you choose, use pure extract, not imitation.

To cook with real vanilla beans, start by looking for beans that are thick and tough but pliable. Pound or rub the bean gently, to crush the millions of inner seeds and release the oils, before splitting it lengthwise. Flatten each half bean, inside up, and using the tip of a small knife, scrape out the seeds, and deposit them into your recipe. Once scraped, the spent pods can be stored in sugar to harness as much of the oil as possible. (Then use that vanilla sugar in coffee, tea, or sprinkled on your sugar cookies!) I also macerate my spent pods in rum, which, after a time, becomes my own homemade extract.

Vanilla can be bought in several forms: as a bean (look for bargains online); as a paste, which is concentrated extract with added seeds; in powdered form, which is made from ground-up dried pods; as an extract, which is the most common form; and as an imitation extract, which is to be avoided by all right-thinking people.

VANILLA-TOMATO: Just calm down. Tomato is a fruit, after all, and in much of the world, including France, there are some great tomato dessert applications, including this one. Take 2 peeled ripe tomatoes (really ripe—this is non-negotiable), and cook in a skillet with 1 tablespoon of sugar, stirring occasionally, until the liquid has evaporated and the sugar has caramelized. Remove from the skillet and cool completely. Add the cooled tomato to the vanilla milk base, and proceed as directed. This ice cream is especially nice with a drizzle of caramel sauce.

VANILLA-LOBSTER: Vanilla and tomato look pretty normal now, don't they? Only the most open-minded of you cooks will attempt this, I know. But I know you are out there, so this is for you. Fresh, sweet, succulent lobster is made even more delectable with vanilla. Sauté chunks of fresh, raw lobster tail in unsalted butter, a tablespoon of sugar, and ½ of a scraped vanilla bean. Cool completely. Make the vanilla ice cream base above with the addition of the finely grated zest of 1 lemon. Chop the cooled lobster into small chunks and fold into the base. Freeze as directed. Serve with buttery vanilla shortbread, tuile cookies, vanilla caramel glaze, or tropical fruit salsa.

VANILLA-ADZUKI BEAN: Red adzuki beans are a dessert filling and flavoring that originated in Japan, but have spread throughout Asia, and have become a favorite ingredient in Hawaiian shaved ice. They are available in Asian markets, whole and dried, as a presweetened paste, or precooked whole in cans (which is the easiest way to use them). Add ½ cup of sweetened beans to the base before the cream is folded in. Serve with sesame candies, coconut macaroons, or sprinkle it with Li Hing Mui powder (pulverized dried, salted plums) like they do in Hawaii. *Mahalo.*

SPRINKLE POPS: Roll mini scoops of vanilla in a dish of sprinkles, spear with tiny spoons, and freeze them solid. Then hand them out and prepare for smiles.

chocolate ice cream

MAKES ABOUT 1 QUART OF ICE CREAM

I prefer my chocolate ice cream deep and dark. If you prefer yours a touch milkier, you can omit the cocoa powder. If you like it even darker, substitute unsweetened chocolate for half of the bittersweet chocolate.

INGREDIENTS

1 cup bittersweet chocolate, chopped (or bittersweet chocolate chips)

1 cup milk

One 13-ounce can sweetened condensed milk

1 teaspoon pure vanilla extract

1 tablespoon unsweetened cocoa powder

1 tablespoon fresh lemon juice

Pinch of salt

2 cups heavy cream

METHOD

1. Place the chopped chocolate in a large bowl. Bring the milk to a near boil, then pour it over the chopped chocolate. Let sit for 5 minutes, then stir until smooth.

2. Stir in sweetened condensed milk, vanilla, cocoa powder, lemon juice, and salt.

3. In a separate bowl, whip the heavy cream until it reaches soft peak. Fold the cream gently into the chocolate milk mixture, then transfer to a shallow freezable container.

4. Cover with plastic wrap or waxed paper pressed directly on the surface of the ice cream, and place in the freezer for 6 hours.

5. Scoop and serve the ice cream with fresh berries, whipped cream, bitter orange caramel, a sprinkle of fancy salt (see Salt, page 6), or crushed Hawaiian-style potato chips. That's what I said.

VARIATIONS

EXTRA-BITTER CHOCOLATE: Adding coffee to chocolate doesn't necessarily make it "mocha." Sometimes, that extra hit of bitterness just emphasizes the bitter qualities of the chocolate. Replace the vanilla extract with a teaspoon of instant espresso powder, coffee extract, or a shot of espresso.

MOCHA: If mocha is what you're looking for, then amp up the joe. In addition to the vanilla extract, add ¼ cup of instant espresso powder, or 2 tablespoons of coffee extract.

Chocolate Ice Cream

MILK CHOCOLATE: Some people prefer the gentler chocolate. If that's you, omit the cocoa powder and replace the bittersweet with milk chocolate.

GIANDUJA: This Italian entry into the roll call of deliciousness combines milk chocolate and hazelnut paste. It is not dissimilar to Nutella (another Italian invention). You can use gianduja as you would the milk chocolate variation above, or make the recipe with Nutella in place of chocolate. (You can also use the recipe on page 81 for Gianduja Gelato.)

CHOCOLATE-BACON: It's a little hipster, I know, but there is a reason so many people like it. Salt, smoke, and chocolate complement each other perfectly. You can simply sprinkle bacon over your finished chocolate ice cream, or infuse the flavor within. Fry chopped bacon until it is very crispy, but be careful not to burn it. Remove from the heat, pour off the excess fat,

CHOCOLATE

Chocolate has a sexy history, which perfectly illustrates Western civilization's finders-keepers mentality. The Spanish came upon the cocoa tree, which had been flourishing in the tropics of the Americas for centuries, and was used for both food and currency. Moctezuma had amassed a chocolaty fortune by the time Cortés arrived.

It was discovered long ago (probably on a dare) that cocoa beans on the ground, rotting in the sun, tasted better than the freshly plucked ones. Fermented, roasted, shelled, and ground, the bean paste was mixed with water and spices into a sludgy but delicious drink called *xocolatl* (which means "bitter water"). The Spanish recorded this practice in great detail, including the drink's stimulating quality. Cortés noted that one cup kept his soldiers fresh for the entire day. All the better to conquer you with.

When cocoa hit Europe, it was a rock star. Dandies in powdered wigs drank cocoa seasoned with fashionable spices, and chocolate shops popped up like Starbucks. But it was not until the mid-nineteenth century that the clever Swiss processed chocolate into candy. Made with the addition of more cocoa butter (extracted from the bean during grinding), milk (for milk chocolate), vanilla, and varying degrees of sugar (for semisweet, bittersweet, etc.), the complication of making chocolate is only surpassed by the complication of choosing one. My general rule is to cook with what you like to eat. Most recipes in this book will call for bittersweet, but you can feel free to substitute your preferred level of "cocoa-ness."

then immediately add the cup of milk. Stir, scraping the delicious crusty bits off the bottom of the pan, then set aside to cool completely. Follow the recipe as directed, using this bacon milk in place of the regular milk. (That is probably the first and last time you will hear the phrase "bacon milk.")

CHOCOLATE-GOAT CHEESE: Another entry for the adventurous cooks. Goat cheese varies in intensity from slightly acidic to supergamey. The more pungent cheese will hold up to a darker chocolate, but I prefer the lighter varieties. I like ice cream to be delicious first, and unusual second. Made well, chocolate ice cream with a subtle goaty flavor will cause you to ponder your mouth for a minute before identifying with delight its ingredients. To the above recipe stir in ¼ cup of mild goat cheese before the whipped cream is folded in.

Chocolate-Cardamom Ice Cream
(recipe on page 74)

strawberry ice cream

MAKES ABOUT 1 QUART OF ICE CREAM

This basic recipe also works wonderfully when made with raspberries, blackberries, peaches, nectarines, plums, apricots, or cherries.

INGREDIENTS

3 cups sliced ripe strawberries

¼ cup water

Finely grated zest of 1 lemon

1 tablespoon fresh lemon juice

One 13-ounce can sweetened condensed milk

1 cup milk

1 vanilla bean, split

1 cup strawberry jam (store-bought or homemade)

Pinch of salt

2 cups heavy cream

METHOD

1. Combine the berries, water, zest, and juice in a small saucepan over medium heat. Cook, stirring occasionally, until the berries release their liquid. Continue cooking until the berries break down, the liquid evaporates, and the mixture becomes jammy. Remove from the heat and cool completely.

2. In a large bowl, combine the sweetened condensed milk, milk, vanilla bean, strawberry jam, and salt.

3. In a separate bowl, whip the heavy cream until it reaches soft peak. Fold in the strawberry mixture, and transfer to a shallow freezable container.

4. Cover with plastic wrap or waxed paper pressed directly on the surface of the ice cream mixture, and place in the freezer for 6 hours.

5. Scoop and serve with fresh berries, crème fraîche, toasted almonds, chocolate sauce, or a drizzle of reduced balsamic vinegar.

VARIATIONS

MARMALADE: Use the same recipe with your favorite sweet or bitter orange marmalade. Use orange zest and juice in place of the lemon, and pump up the orange flavor with a drop of orange oil, orange flower water, or Grand Marnier.

STRAWBERRY-BALSAMIC: This classic pair is probably overdone, but there is a reason. Add 2 tablespoons of extra-thick or reduced regular balsamic vinegar to the strawberry

Strawberry Ice Cream with balsamic glaze

mixture before the cream is folded in. (Boil 1 cup of regular balsamic vinegar until it is thick and reduced by half; measure your 2 tablespoons from here, and save the rest to drizzle over good French bread or grilled fish.) For added interest, stir in ¼ cup of goat cheese.

STRAWBERRY-SOUR CREAM: Strawberries dipped in sour cream and rolled in brown sugar were a favorite childhood treat. To re-create this, replace the milk with an equal amount of sour cream, and serve it with a sprinkle of brown sugar, or a drizzle of caramel sauce.

STRAWBERRY-CHEESECAKE: Add 4 ounces of cream cheese to the strawberry mixture before the cream is folded in. To complete the effect, serve with a sprinkle of crushed graham cracker crumbs, and a dollop of crème fraîche or sour cream.

STRAWBERRY

Strawberries used to be a special thing, until airplanes made it possible to have them anywhere at any time. This fact has, for me, taken the bloom off the rose. There is really nothing interesting about your typical strawberry. But, when I can find fresh, local, seasonal strawberries, or better yet, *fraises de bois*, then I am all-in.

Strawberry ice cream is a hard thing to do well. The problem is that it is either too fresh, or too fake. The folding in of fresh berries, which are comprised mainly of sweet juicy water, inevitably results in strawberry-shaped ice chunks. The addition of a simple puree of berries adds mostly water, too. But the use of extracts is always obviously artificial. The answer? Cook out the water from the berries first. Mischief managed.

HOMEMADE JAM

To make your own stovetop jam, combine 2 cups of cleaned berries or stone fruit with 2 tablespoons of sugar, a teaspoon of fresh lemon juice and a pinch of salt. Cook over high heat, stirring, until the fruit's liquid starts to exude. Continue cooking and stirring until the liquid has evaporated, and the mixture has thickened to jam consistency. Remove from the heat, and adjust its sweetness with more sugar if necessary. (Every fruit, every crop has different sugar levels, so the exact amount of sugar will always be to taste.) Cool this completely before stirring it into your ice cream base. For fast cooling, spread it out onto a baking sheet and place it in the freezer for 15 minutes.

mint chip ice cream

MAKES ABOUT 1 QUART OF ICE CREAM

Most mint chip ice cream found in the world is green. But not all, and there is something to be said for a white pepperminty frozen delight. That said, a little green can be fun, too. Feel free to use or omit the food coloring at your own discretion. See page 149 for Variations.

INGREDIENTS

One 13-ounce can sweetened condensed milk

1 cup milk

2 to 3 drops peppermint mint extract

1 to 2 drops green food coloring (optional)

1 tablespoon fresh lemon juice

Pinch of salt

2 cups heavy cream

1 cup chopped dark chocolate or mini chips

METHOD

1. In a large bowl, combine the sweetened condensed milk, milk, peppermint extract, food coloring (if desired), lemon juice, and salt.

2. In a separate bowl, whip the heavy cream until it reaches soft peak. Fold in the mint mixture and the chocolate, then transfer to a shallow freezable container.

3. Cover with plastic wrap or waxed paper pressed directly on the surface of the ice cream, and place in the freezer for 6 hours.

4. Scoop and serve with chocolate sauce, or a drizzle of your best bourbon.

MINT

I am a firm believer in mint. There are multiple varieties with distinct differences. Spearmint is the most commonly available fresh mint, but it is not the most delicious. I prefer fresh peppermint, when I can get my hands on it. If not, I stick to peppermint extract or oil, which is easier to obtain and use, hence its inclusion in the following recipe.

For those interested, fresh mint ice cream is a cinch. Wash and stem 1 cup of fresh mint leaves. Chop them finely, combine them with milk, and warm in the microwave for 30 to 60 seconds. Set aside at room temperature to steep and cool completely. Drain out leaves, and use the infused milk in the recipe as directed. When using real mint, I prefer to opt out of the food coloring. *Au naturel*, baby!

Orange Peppermint with Chocolate Chips Ice Cream

(recipe on page 149)

coffee ice cream

MAKES ABOUT 1 QUART OF ICE CREAM

Instant espresso powder, available in most supermarkets, is my favorite instant coffee. It is bitter and dark, and tastes like real coffee. When in doubt, I follow my coffee mantra—"If it's not good enough to drink, it's not good enough to cook with it." This is, coincidentally, also my wine mantra.

INGREDIENTS

1 cup milk

3 tablespoons instant espresso powder, or coffee extract

One 13-ounce can sweetened condensed milk

½ vanilla bean, scraped

2 teaspoons fresh lemon juice

Pinch of salt

2 cups heavy cream

METHOD

1. Warm the cup of milk in the microwave for 30 to 60 seconds. Add the instant espresso and set it aside to steep and cool completely.

2. In a large bowl, combine the coffee milk, sweetened condensed milk, vanilla bean, lemon juice, and salt.

3. In a separate bowl, whip the heavy cream until it reaches soft peak. Fold the cream gently into the coffee mixture, then transfer to a shallow freezable container.

4. Cover with plastic wrap or waxed paper pressed directly on the surface of the ice cream, and place in the freezer for 6 hours.

5. Scoop and serve with chocolate sauce, caramel sauce, crushed toffee, coffee crunch, chocolate shavings, or a shot of Irish whiskey.

VARIATIONS

COFFEE-CINNAMON: What works for your café latte will work for your ice cream too! Add to the steeping coffee milk ½ teaspoon of ground cinnamon, or 1 crushed whole stick. Let it cool and proceed with the recipe as directed.

COFFEE-CARDAMOM: Arabic coffee has included cardamom seeds in varying degrees for centuries. Some coffeehouses in London mix them in equal parts, which seems a bit too strong for this dessert application. Try adding 5 to 6 crushed pods with the steeping coffee milk, then proceed with the recipe as directed.

COFFEE-ORANGE: The combination is great at breakfast, so why not after dinner? Add the finely grated zest of 2 oranges to the steeping coffee milk, then proceed with the recipe as directed.

COFFEE

Coffee ice cream has been my all-time favorite flavor since I was a little kid. Looking back, I can see that it was a gateway to the full-blown caffeine addiction I currently enjoy. (And I do mean *enjoy*.) To achieve great coffee ice cream, it's best to start with great coffee. If time allows, grind your beans as finely as possible and steep them in warm milk. When cool, strain out the coffee grounds through a fine-mesh strainer lined with cheesecloth. There will be a few stray grounds, but they are not offensive and indicate the use of real coffee. (Insomniacs can relax—this works just as well with decaffeinated beans, too.)

But because finding great beans, and spending the time to grind and steep them, is not always possible, this recipe uses the next best method, great instant coffee powder. (Yes, such a thing exists.) There is also such a thing as good coffee extract, which can be found at better "gourmet" food stores.

coconut ice cream

MAKES ABOUT 1 QUART OF ICE CREAM

If you can get a fresh coconut, by all means do so. To remove the husk, smash it on the ground outside (the driveway is best), with a bucket nearby to catch the coconut water. (It makes great rice!) Once cracked, use an oyster shucker or screwdriver to break it into pieces, and remove the white meat. I like to keep the thin brown inner skin when I grate fresh coconut. It's not offensive to my palate, and it lets everyone know I used the fresh nut.

INGREDIENTS

1 cup unsweetened grated or shredded coconut

One 13-ounce can sweetened condensed milk

1 cup canned unsweetened coconut milk

½ teaspoon coconut extract

1 tablespoon fresh lemon juice

Pinch of salt

2 cups heavy cream

METHOD

1. Preheat the oven to 375°F. Spread the coconut out on a rimmed baking sheet and toast in the oven until golden brown, stirring periodically, about 10 minutes.

2. Warm the sweetened condensed milk and coconut milk together in the microwave or on the stovetop. When the coconut is toasted, add it hot to the milk mixture and set aside to steep and cool. Add the coconut extract, lemon juice, and salt. (If this can be done the night before, the coconut flavor will be even more intense.) When cool, strain out the coconut. Be sure to press out all the delicious coconut-flavored liquids.

3. In a separate bowl, whip the heavy cream until it reaches soft peak. Fold the cream gently into the coconut mixture, then transfer to a shallow freezable container.

4. Cover with plastic wrap or waxed paper pressed directly on the surface of the ice cream, and place in the freezer for 6 hours.

5. Scoop and serve with chocolate sauce, caramel-rum sauce, grilled pineapple, toasted macadamia nuts, pumpkin-seed brittle, or a shot of Malibu Rum.

COCONUT-LIME: Add the finely grated zest of 1 lime, and replace the lemon juice with lime juice for a brighter tropical quality.

CINNAMON-COCONUT: Add a crushed cinnamon stick to the milk with the steep, or add ½ teaspoon of ground cinnamon to the base before the cream is folded in.

COCONUT-CASHEW: Add ½ cup of chopped cashews to the pan of toasting coconut, toast them together, and add them together to the milk mixture.

COCONUT

Helado de coco is my favorite food to get in Mexico. For years I tried to replicate the coco-nutty goodness of Mexican ice cream. I tried coconut milk. I tried desiccated, shredded, and freshly grated coconut. I tried toasting the coconut and steeping it hot from the oven in milk. But nothing was ever as good. Finally, one evening I was honored to work a dinner with Mexican culinary goddess, cookbook author, and restaurateur Chef Patricia Quintana, who is Mexico's Ambassador of Cuisine, and creator of that country's first culinary academy. She helped me properly season Mexican chocolate truffles, showed me the best way to slice a mango, and gave me the secret to helado de coco. It's extract! I still like to toast my coconut, but now I always add a few drops of extract. The combination makes the flavor intense, but surprisingly not artificial.

There are many types of coconut, and any of them will work when making ice cream. Just be sure to pay attention to the sugar content. If your coconut is sweetened, your finished product will be sweeter. An extra squeeze of lime juice can help reduce that effect. For no-churn ice cream that utilizes sweetened condensed milk, I prefer unsweetened coconut, or better yet, fresh grated coconut. I have been known to buy a sack of coconuts, husk and grate them all using my food processor's grating attachment, and freeze the grated coconut in ziptop plastic bags for gradual use throughout the year.

add-ins galore

Anything can be added in to an ice cream. Doing so will alter the texture and flavor, and sometimes (as is the case with alcohol) inhibit the freeze. But just because it will alter your mix is no reason to change your plans. By all means, let's add it in. Here are some things you should know about the addition of various ingredients.

FRUIT ADD-INS

Fruit has water, so to minimize the iciness of your ice cream, you must minimize the water. Chunks of fruit can be folded in, but consider that the longer they are in the freezer, the icier they will become. Eventually they will become little fruity ice cubes, which are not that pleasant to eat. There are four solutions to the icy fruit problem:

1. MAKE A PUREE.

In most cases, if you simply puree the fruit and add it in, you will be adding in water, and the entire recipe will end up too thin and icy. It's better to cook down the fruit and reduce to evaporate as much of the water as possible. This will also intensify the flavor and color. Let this jammy mixture cool, run it through the blender or food processor, and stir it into the milk base before folding in the whipped cream. This will produce an all-over fruit flavor.

There are a couple exceptions to this. Bananas and mangos don't contain much water, so their fresh purees are very thick. Other fruits and vegetable purees that you come across may have similar properties, such as any kind of potato and other root vegetables. (While you might not have thought about vegetable or potato ice cream yet, it pays to know how one would incorporate anything—you wouldn't want to limit your creativity. Keep this in mind later, when we discuss sweet potatoes, beets, and parsnips.) Some fruits are a bad choice for ice cream, because they contain too much water. Any melon, kiwi fruit, and certain tropicals like the dragon fruit have a dramatic change in flavor and color when they are heated and reduced. These fruits are best saved for sorbet or sherbet, where they can be used fresh. (See the Fruit Sauce Cooking Chart, pages 139–41, for a detailed list of what can and cannot be heated.)

2. MAKE A SWIRL.

Make jam, as described on page 23. You can keep it chunky, or cool it and puree it as above. But instead of stirring it into the milk base, layer it with a completed vanilla ice cream base in its freezer container. There is no need to swirl it in with a spoon. When the ice cream is frozen and scooped, it will swirl automatically. You can swirl in other sauces this way, too, as you will see below.

3. FORGET IT.

Make a plain ice cream and serve the fruit on top. This seems like a cop-out, but sometimes it is the best choice. Especially when the fruit is amazing. (Sometimes, it's just not possible to improve on Mother Nature.) For instance, in the winter there are some terrific citrus fruits, like the blood orange. Reducing its juice for your recipe will result in a pink ice cream that is orange flavored, something you could easily achieve with orange juice concentrate and food coloring. You completely lose the impact of this beautiful, dramatic fruit. In such cases, a scoop of ice cream topped with a generous helping of blood orange suprêmes is the best answer. That doesn't mean you don't get to be creative. (No one said it had to be vanilla ice cream under the oranges.) Add orange zest to the ice cream base. Or fresh thyme. Or bay leaves. Or peppercorns. Or toasted coriander seed. Or Grand Marnier. Or do keep it vanilla, but add another layer of flavor in the form of a sauce or garnish. You see how much fun this can be!

4. FOLD IT IN ANYWAY, AND CROSS YOUR FINGERS.

These ice creams are quick to make and quick to freeze and, if you are serving one on the same day you make it, there is a chance the fruit won't have time to freeze into icy chunks. Hey—no guts, no glory.

SWIRL-INS

Anything that is relatively thick can be swirled into an ice cream base. The key is to layer the addition rather than stir it in. Stirring frequently incorporates the flavors and colors too much into the base ice cream, rather than creating ribbons. Start by putting about an inch of ice cream base in the freezer container. Drizzle your desired swirl on top. (See some suggestions below.) Top with another inch of ice cream, then another layer of drizzle, and repeat until you've added all the ice cream. Finish with a drizzle, and freeze as directed. When you scoop your frozen ice cream it will swirl automatically.

For a chocolate swirl, it's best not to add straight melted chocolate, but rather a premade sauce or a melted ganache (see pages 134 to 137). Straight chocolate will freeze solid and will crack rather than swirl (which is one method the big producers use to make chocolate chip ice cream). You can also swirl in a caramel sauce (see page 136), fruit jam, marmalade, or fruit spread.

Finally, why not try swirling in another flavor of ice cream or a sorbet? Don't try to drizzle them. Your brain might explode. Make two separate recipes, freeze each separately, then simply layer alternating scoops in a new freezer container. Freeze the concoction for another hour to help it set and swirl better.

NUTTY ADD-INS

Stirring nuts into something seems so simple you're probably wondering why I am bothering to mention it at all. But you'd be surprised how different good nuts can be. (There is no point in making a joke here. The one in your head is probably better than anything I could write.)

Toasted nuts are far superior to raw nuts. Heat releases the delicious nutty oils, and adds a crisp finish. The proper way to toast nuts is on a rimmed baking sheet in a 350°F oven until they are golden brown and have released their nutty aroma. Some cooks toast nuts in a pan on the stovetop. That is, however, amateur hour. By using that method the only part of the nut that gets toasted is the part touching the pan. Only the oven method can unlock the full nut potential.

One more thing. Cool your toasted nuts completely before folding them into your ice cream base. Stuff doesn't freeze when it's hot (at least not for a very, very long time), and it will mess up the texture of your ice cream. A quick trip to the freezer is sufficient.

COOKIE AND CANDY ADD-INS

Chunks are good, but if they are too big, they are less fun. When they freeze, frozen chunks of candy are a danger to dental work everywhere. Try to keep them the approximate size of a chocolate chip or smaller, if you can.

Avoid adding caramel candies. When caramel freezes it is impossible to eat daintily, and will almost certainly pull out a filling. (Better to opt for a caramel sauce swirl or topping, if caramel is your thing.) Cookies are no problem, but cookie dough is another story. While I have been eating raw cookie dough for years, there are some who will be alarmed at the idea of eating something that includes a raw egg. (Despite the fact that raw eggs have been consumed for centuries, and that more cases of salmonella are contracted from dirty melons than beef, poultry, and eggs combined.) For those of you timid about this, and those of you who work for the health department, it is possible to simply omit the eggs from a cookie dough recipe to achieve a similar effect. To get it into good ice cream add-in form, roll the dough into a thin snake, and cut off small, mini marshmallow–size coins.

warm-weather ice creams

~~~

Up until the twentieth century, there was no seasonal eating, no organic or locavore movements. There was just eating. People ate locally with the seasons because they had no choice. But now, living in the modern world means that we can all eat like kings. And that can be both good and bad. Certainly it makes shopping and menu planning easy. Whatever creative spark you ignite on any given day can easily be fulfilled. But just because you can acquire something out of season doesn't mean it will be any good. Anyone who has ever grown their own tomatoes in the summer knows exactly what I mean.

Eating seasonally just makes sense, both environmentally and economically. But even without the overarching ethical issues, eating seasonally is simply a more joyful way to eat. Each month that rolls around offers something new and delectable that I haven't eaten for a year. Like old friends at a reunion, it's great to see them, until I get sick of them, at which time they will happily disappear.

rosebud ice cream

MAKES ABOUT 1 QUART OF ICE CREAM

Rose water is a great ingredient that I couldn't live without. I add it to custards, cakes, syrups, sauces, and of course, ice cream. Depending on the accompaniments, it can go either in an exotic or Victorian direction. Sure, it's old-fashioned. (But then, so am I.)

INGREDIENTS

2 tablespoons rose water

1 cup milk

One 13-ounce can sweetened condensed milk

Finely grated zest of 1 lemon

1 tablespoon fresh lemon juice

Pinch of salt

2 cups heavy cream

2 tablespoons finely crushed dried rosebuds or petals

METHOD

1. In a large bowl, combine the rose water, milk, sweetened condensed milk, lemon zest, lemon juice, and salt.

2. In a separate bowl, whip the heavy cream until it reaches soft peak. Fold the cream and crushed rosebuds gently into the rose mixture, then transfer to a shallow freezable container.

3. Cover the ice cream with plastic wrap or waxed paper pressed directly on the surface of the ice cream, and place in the freezer for 6 hours.

4. Scoop and serve with vanilla pound cake, baklava, madeleines, sesame seed tuiles, fresh berries, or stone fruits.

VARIATIONS

ROSE-SAFFRON: For a Middle Eastern twist, toast 3 to 4 strands of saffron in a hot dry skillet for a few seconds until they crisp up. Remove from the heat immediately and let cool, then crush and add to the 1 cup of milk. Warm in the microwave for 30 to 60 seconds, set aside to steep and cool, then proceed with the recipe as directed.

PISTACHIO-ROSE: Toast 1 cup of shelled pistachio nuts, cool completely, then chop them very finely, and fold them into the rose base with the whipped cream.

Rosebud Ice Cream

strawberry-rhubarb ice cream

MAKES ABOUT 1 QUART OF ICE CREAM

Rhubarb's classic partner is the strawberry. Sweet and tart are commonly paired, and rhubarb not only benefits from, but screams for, a sweet pairing. Really ripe rhubarb is said to have subtle strawberry overtones. All I know is that these two flavors just make me smile. I have always been a fan of rhubarb in any form, my favorite preparation being a stalk pulled directly from the garden and dipped in sugar the way we ate it when we were kids. This recipe blends them in the classic sense, but there are a number of ways these flavors can be combined in a frozen dessert, as you will notice in the Variations section opposite.

INGREDIENTS

2 cups cleaned and diced fresh rhubarb

2 pints strawberries

1 tablespoon sugar

Finely grated zest of 1 lemon

1 teaspoon fresh lemon juice

One 13-ounce can sweetened condensed milk

1 cup milk

½ vanilla bean, scraped, or 1 teaspoon pure vanilla extract

Pinch of salt

2 cups heavy cream

METHOD

1. Combine the rhubarb, strawberries, sugar, lemon zest and juice in a medium saucepan over medium heat. Cook, stirring occasionally, until the fruit softens, exudes its liquid, and then takes on a jammy consistency. Remove from the heat and set aside to cool completely.

2. In a large bowl, combine the cooled rhubarb-strawberry jam, sweetened condensed milk, milk, vanilla, and salt and mix thoroughly.

3. In a separate bowl, whip the heavy cream until it reaches soft peak. Fold the cream gently into the strawberry-rhubarb mixture, then transfer to a shallow freezable container.

4. Cover the ice cream with plastic wrap or waxed paper pressed directly on the surface of the ice cream, and place in the freezer for 6 hours.

5. Scoop and serve with fresh strawberries, orange suprêmes, whipped cream, toasted almonds, oatmeal cookies, or cardamom shortbread.

THE SWIRL: Make two separate jams, and mix only the rhubarb jam into the milk base before adding the whipped cream. Scoop 1 inch of the rhubarb mixture into a shallow freezable container. Drizzle some strawberry jam on top, and repeat using all the rhubarb and strawberry components.

OTHER BERRIES: Try the same recipe with sweet, ripe raspberries, blueberries, or blackberries.

RHUBARB-ROSEMARY: Rosemary's piney overtones work magic on tart rhubarb. Finely chop 2 tablespoons of rosemary needles (I like to use a spice mill or coffee grinder), then add them to the rhubarb jam preparations. You can omit the strawberry, or leave it in, as it works well with rosemary, too.

RHUBARB, HONEY, GINGER, AND CARDAMOM: This is one of my favorite blends. Omit the strawberries, replace the sugar with ¾ cup honey, and add to the jam mixture 1 grated knuckle of peeled fresh ginger and ½ teaspoon ground cardamom.

RHUBARB AND SAFFRON: This precious spice adds a unique earthy and exotic depth of flavor to tart rhubarb. Toast 3 to 4 strands of saffron in a hot dry skillet for a few seconds until they crisp up. Remove from the pan immediately and let cool, then crush and add to the 1 cup of milk. Warm in the microwave for 30 to 60 seconds, then set aside to steep and cool. Omit the strawberries, then proceed with the recipe as directed.

RHUBARB

Rhubarb is an easy plant to cultivate, which explains its surge in popularity in victory gardens during World War II. It looks like thick red celery, and it is the red celerylike stalks that we eat. Stay away from the leaves, as they contain high levels of oxalic acid, which is toxic—a fact discovered during World War II when it was suggested that people eat the rhubarb leaves as a substitute for vegetables made unavailable by the war. It takes quite a lot of rhubarb leaves to cause serious damage, but a little nibble of leaf will produce a wicked tummy ache.

summer berry ice cream

MAKES ABOUT 1 QUART OF ICE CREAM

When the ripe berries show up in the market, I grab them—even if I have no intention of using them right away. Frozen in ziptop plastic bags, they'll keep for months at their peak of season freshness. This recipe works for whichever sweet, juicy ripe berry you can lay your hands on. Or use all of them in a "summer mix." See page 149 for more Variations.

INGREDIENTS

3 cups berries

¼ cup water

Finely grated zest of 1 lemon

1 tablespoon fresh lemon juice

One 13-ounce can sweetened condensed milk

1 cup milk

½ vanilla bean, scraped, or 1 teaspoon pure vanilla extract

Pinch of salt

2 cups heavy cream

METHOD

1. Combine the berries, water, zest, and juice in a small saucepan over medium heat. Cook, stirring occasionally, until the berries release their liquid. Continue cooking until the berries break down, the liquid evaporates, and the mixture becomes jammy. Remove from the heat and cool completely.

2. Puree the cooled jam, either by passing through a fine mesh strainer, or running it through a food processor or blender. (If you are looking for a very refined finished product, you may choose at this point to strain out the seeds.)

3. In a large bowl, combine the cooled berry jam, sweetened condensed milk, milk, vanilla bean, and salt and mix thoroughly.

4. In a separate bowl, whip the heavy cream until it reaches soft peak. Fold the cream gently into the berry mixture, then transfer to a shallow freezable container.

5. Cover the ice cream with plastic wrap or waxed paper pressed directly on the surface of the ice cream, and place in the freezer for 6 hours.

6. Scoop and serve with whipped cream, fresh berries, warm berry-basil compote, citrus suprême salsa, toasted almonds, or lemon tuile cookies.

RASPBERRY OR BLACKBERRY GOAT CHEESE: This magical mix is easily made by replacing ½ cup of the milk with ½ cup of mild goat cheese. Use a more pungent cheese for true goat fans. Two tablespoons of finely chopped spearmint make a nice herbal addition.

BLUEBERRY-BLUE CHEESE: Stir 2 to 3 tablespoons of Stilton, Gorgonzola, or a Maytag blue in with the jam while it's warm; it will melt and macerate nicely. Taste your base carefully before adding salt, as these cheeses are already highly salted. Also, I often find it necessary to increase the acid by another teaspoon of lemon juice, but that all depends on the ripeness of both the berries and the cheese.

BERRY-BASIL: Perhaps my favorite herb pairing of all time, basil and berries are exotically herbaceous and floral. Add ¼ cup chopped fresh basil to the jam as it cooks. If I can find it, opal basil is my favorite, followed next by Thai basil. Regular Italian basil works, too, although it contains less of the anise-qualities that I love in other basil varieties.

Blueberry–Blue Cheese Ice Cream

cherry-chocolate ice cream

MAKES ABOUT 1 QUART OF ICE CREAM

This flavor is an oldie but a goody. In cake form it is known as Black Forest (Schwarzwalder Kirschtorte), because the Black Forest (Schwarzwälder) region of Bavaria is known for its wild cherries. But of course, in the world of ice cream, we have two guys from Vermont and the Grateful Dead to thank. See pages 149–50 for Variations.

INGREDIENTS

3 cups fresh cherries, halved and pitted

1 tablespoon kirschwasser

1 tablespoon sugar

Finely grated zest and juice of 1 lemon

1 cup bittersweet chocolate, chopped (or bittersweet chocolate chips)

One 13-ounce can sweetened condensed milk

½ cup milk

2 tablespoons unsweetened cocoa powder

Pinch of salt

2 cups heavy cream

METHOD

1. Combine the cherries with the kirschwasser, sugar, and lemon and toss to combine. Set aside for at least 60 minutes to macerate. (Overnight is better.)

2. In a ceramic or glass bowl, melt the chocolate in the microwave for 10- to 20-second increments, stirring in between, until it is completely melted. Slowly stir in the sweetened condensed milk, milk, cocoa powder, salt, and the strained juices from the macerating cherries.

3. In a separate bowl, whip the heavy cream until it reaches soft peak. Fold the cream gently into the chocolate base, then transfer half the mixture to a shallow freezable container. Sprinkle on half the cherries, cover with the remaining ice cream mixture, and finish by sprinkling on the remaining cherries. The ice cream will swirl itself when you scoop it.

4. Cover with plastic wrap or waxed paper pressed directly on the surface of the ice cream, and place it in the freezer for 6 hours.

5. Scoop and serve with a dollop of whipped cream, chocolate curls or shavings, fresh cherries, or a splash of kirschwasser.

PITTING CHERRIES

Pitting cherries by hand is easy, but messy. The first time I did it, the mechanical pitter I used became cumbersome, so I simply started pinching them in half with my bare hands to release the pit. Deeply stained cherry hands take a little over a week to de-stain. Use rubber gloves, or invest in a good pitter. If you have a lot of cherries, pit them all, and freeze in ziptop plastic bags.

Cherry-Chocolate Ice Cream

peach ice cream

MAKES ABOUT 1 QUART OF ICE CREAM

A good peach is a rare treat. Too often I find them served out of a can, or fresh but under-ripe. This is so common that unless you come from peach country, a good, fresh, ripe peach—a little tart, but sweet and juicy—is unknown to most people. So when I do find them, after eating my fill of them fresh, ice cream is the next item on my peach agenda. See page 150 for more Variations.

INGREDIENTS

3 large fresh peaches, sliced

¼ cup water

Finely grated zest of 1 lemon

1 tablespoon fresh lemon juice

Pinch of salt

1/8 teaspoon freshly grated nutmeg

One 13-ounce can sweetened condensed milk

1 cup milk

2 cups heavy cream

METHOD

1. Combine the peaches, water, zest, juice, and salt in a small saucepan over medium heat. Cook, stirring occasionally, until the peaches release their liquid. Continue cooking until the fruit breaks down, the liquid evaporates, and the mixture becomes jammy. Remove from the heat and cool completely.

2. Puree the cooled peaches, either by passing through a fine mesh strainer, or running through a food processor or blender. If you find little bits of peach skin unsightly, pass the puree through a fine-mesh strainer.

3. In a large bowl, combine the peach puree, nutmeg, sweetened condensed milk, and milk.

4. In a separate bowl, whip the heavy cream until it reaches soft peak. Fold the cream into the peach mixture, then transfer to a shallow freezable container.

5. Cover with plastic wrap or waxed paper pressed directly on the surface of the ice cream, and place it in the freezer for 6 hours.

6. Scoop and serve with whipped cream, fresh sliced peaches, pecan-caramel sauce, candied ginger sauce, fresh berry-basil compote, pecan sandies, or Mexican wedding cookies.

PEACH-BASIL: Another delightful use for basil. Macerate the peaches with ½ cup of chopped fresh basil and 1 tablespoon of sugar for 1 hour before pureeing. Try it with tarragon, too.

PEACH-PROSCIUTTO: If you can have bacon with chocolate, why not really good, smoky, salty ham with peaches? Shave some good prosciutto, Parma, or other delectable smoky ham very thinly, then chop it finely and fold it in with the whipped cream. Then when it's ready, try it with a drizzle of pecan-caramel sauce and a fried prosciutto chip. Wow.

Peach-Prosciutto Ice Cream with fried prosciutto chips

PEACH PEEL

I do not typically bother peeling my peaches (or other stone fruits for that matter). I do not find their skin terribly offensive to the palate, and I think it helps give my ice cream a fresh, homemade quality. But if you are a peeler, here's how to do it properly: Boil a pot of water, and have a bowl of ice water at the ready. Cut an "x" at the bottom of the peach. (That's the opposite of the stem end.) Blanch the peach for 25 to 30 seconds in the boiling water, then transfer them directly to the ice bath. When cool, the skin will fall right off. If it doesn't, your peaches were under-ripe.

pineapple-pepper ice cream

MAKES ABOUT 1 QUART OF ICE CREAM

The sweet, tart, hot combination of pineapple and pepper is the epitome of zesty. Black pepper is perfectly delicious here, but if you have pink peppercorns, use them. They are not only a little more complex, but also have a pretty color. Of course, if you are spice-shy, omit the pepper altogether and make do with deliciously plain pineapple ice cream. See page 150 for Variations.

INGREDIENTS

1 tablespoon (½ ounce) unsalted butter

3 cups pineapple, cut into small chunks

1 tablespoon molasses

1 tablespoon crushed black or pink peppercorns

One 13-ounce can sweetened condensed milk

1 cup milk

1 tablespoon fresh lime juice

Pinch of salt

2 cups heavy cream

METHOD

1. Melt the butter in a large sauté pan over high heat. Add the pineapple and molasses and cook, stirring frequently, until the natural liquids begin to exude. Reduce the heat, stir in the peppercorns, and continue to cook until the pineapple has softened and caramelized.

2. Remove from the heat and set aside to cool a bit. Puree the cooled pineapple in a blender until smooth, then pass through a fine-mesh strainer to remove excess fiber.

3. In a large bowl, combine the cooled pineapple puree, sweetened condensed milk, milk, lime juice, and salt.

4. In a separate bowl, whip the heavy cream until it reaches soft peak. Fold the cream gently into the pineapple base, then transfer the mixture to a shallow freezable container.

5. Cover with plastic wrap or waxed paper pressed directly on the surface of the ice cream, and place it in the freezer for 6 hours.

6. Scoop and serve with coconut whipped cream, fresh tropical fruit salsa, caramel sauce, caramel-rum glaze, walnut lace cookies, or coconut macaroons.

Pineapple-Pepper Ice Cream

lavender ice cream

Although dried lavender is available year-round, it definitely has a springy feel. Use the purple buds rather than the leaves or stems, as they have a little more pine than floral essence. If you don't have a local lavender gardener, you can get big bags of buds online from any number of lavender farms around the country. See page 150 for more Variations.

INGREDIENTS

1 cup milk

3 tablespoons lavender buds

One 13-ounce can sweetened condensed milk

Finely grated zest of 1 lemon

1 tablespoon fresh lemon juice

Pinch of salt

2 cups heavy cream

METHOD

1. Warm the milk and lavender buds together in the microwave for 30 to 60 seconds. Set aside to steep and cool completely, then strain off the buds.

2. In a large bowl, combine the lavender milk, sweetened condensed milk, lemon zest, lemon juice, and salt.

3. In a separate bowl, whip the heavy cream until it reaches soft peak. Fold the cream gently into the lavender mixture, then transfer to a shallow freezable container.

4. Cover the ice cream with plastic wrap or waxed paper pressed directly on the surface of the ice cream, and place in the freezer for 6 hours.

5. Scoop and serve with fresh berries, peaches, apricots, lavender-caramel sauce, almond toffee, or chopped toasted almonds.

VARIATIONS

LAVENDER-ALMOND: Almond works wonderfully with floral flavors, and lavender is no exception. Replace the cup of milk with almond milk, and fold in ½ cup crushed toasted almonds with the whipped cream. This version is not bad with a shot of amaretto, too.

LAVENDER-PURPLE POTATO: I LOVE this ice cream. The recipe is a variation of Sweet Potato–Marshmallow Swirl ice cream on page 70, but I mention it here for the lavender lovers.

Lavender Ice Cream with
lavender meringues

orange flower water–almond ice cream

Tropically floral orange flower water is usually reserved for the bartender. But a few pastry chefs have discovered its charms, and you find it occasionally in cakes, syrups, and sauces. I particularly love it paired with almond, as the toasty notes really help this flower juice sparkle. See pages 150–51 for another Variation.

INGREDIENTS

2 tablespoons orange flower water

1 cup almond milk

One 13-ounce can sweetened condensed milk

Finely grated zest of 1 orange

1 tablespoon fresh lemon juice

Pinch of salt

2 cups heavy cream

METHOD

1. In a large bowl, combine the orange flower water, almond milk, sweetened condensed milk, orange zest, lemon juice, and salt.

2. In a separate bowl, whip the heavy cream until it reaches soft peak. Fold the cream gently into the orange flower–almond mixture, then transfer to a shallow freezable container.

3. Cover with plastic wrap or waxed paper pressed directly on the surface of the ice cream, and place in the freezer for 6 hours.

4. Scoop and serve over a slice of warm bread pudding, sandwiched between two almond croissants, or topped with citrus suprêmes, sautéed peaches or apricots, or a drizzle of warm chocolate fudge sauce.

VARIATIONS

ORANGE FLOWER–MARZIPAN: Chop marzipan candy into very small bits, toss with some crushed almonds, and fold into the base with the whipped cream.

MARMALADE: A swirl of your favorite bitter or sweet marmalade is delightful with this ice cream. Top an inch of ice cream with a thin layer of marmalade, add another inch of ice cream, more marmalade, etc., until your freezer container is full. The ice cream will swirl itself when you scoop it. Try it with a good strawberry or raspberry jam, too.

key lime ice cream

MAKES ABOUT 1 QUART OF ICE CREAM

The key lime is a cute little fruit. It is smaller than the standard lime, and is sold as the Mexican lime in some parts of the country. The tart, sweet quality of the key lime is to limes what the Meyer lemon is to lemons—less harsh, less tight, less zingy, less acidic, but juicy, rich, and full of flavor. The key lime is yellow when ripe, so don't be fooled by your own sense of logic. See page 151 for another Variation.

INGREDIENTS

¾ cup key lime juice

Finely grated zest of 2 limes

Pinch of kosher salt

One 13-ounce can sweetened condensed milk

1 cup milk

2 cups heavy cream

METHOD

1. In a large bowl, combine the lime juice, zest, salt, and sweetened condensed milk. Slowly stir in the milk.

2. In a separate bowl, whip the heavy cream until it reaches soft peak. Fold the cream into the lime base, then transfer the mixture to a shallow freezable container.

3. Cover with plastic wrap or waxed paper pressed directly on the surface of the ice cream, and place it in the freezer for 6 hours.

4. Scoop and serve with coconut whipped cream, fresh mango-pineapple salsa, watermelon-mint salsa, white chocolate sauce, macadamia nut brittle, or coconut macaroons.

VARIATIONS

MANGO-LIME: Omit the milk, and add 2 cups of ripe mango, pureed in a blender, in its place. You can do the same with guava or papaya.

LIME, MINT, AND GOAT CHEESE: Pungent goat cheese blooms bright with key lime. Substitute a cup of mild goat cheese for the milk, and fold in 2 tablespoons of finely chopped fresh mint.

KEY LIME PIE: For the unmistakable sensation of eating a really cold pie, swirl the ice cream base with crumbled graham cracker crust, and serve with whipped cream.

cold-weather
ice creams

~~~~~

Some flavors just don't go with summer. You can probably find them. You can probably even make them. But they just don't fit. That's probably because we intuitively know that their season is fall or winter, and that their flavors will be more satisfying then. So check the calendar, then proceed with the following chapter.

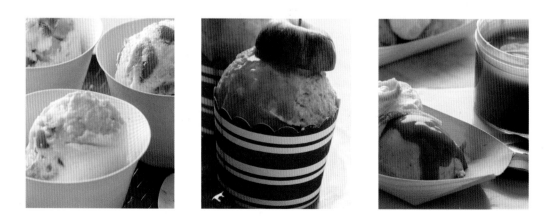

peppermint stick crunch
ice cream

MAKES ABOUT 1 QUART OF ICE CREAM

This ice cream is the epitome of Christmas. It is the one time of year that peppermint sticks flood the market. The hardest part of this recipe is unwrapping the peppermint sticks. If you have forethought, use the round "star mints," or King Leo brand straight sticks, rather than the hooked candy canes, which are notoriously difficult to unwrap. You can crush them using a plastic bag and a mallet, although I much prefer using a food processor. It makes a god-awful sound, and can render the mints too powdery, but it is less messy. I reserve the bigger chunks for the fold-in, and use the finer bits for the milk portion of the recipe. See page 151 for Variations.

INGREDIENTS

1 cup milk

2 cups of crushed peppermint sticks

1 tablespoon pure vanilla extract

One 13-ounce can sweetened condensed milk

1 tablespoon fresh lemon juice

Pinch of salt

2 cups heavy cream

METHOD

1. Place the milk in a small saucepan and bring it to a boil. When it is at the boil, remove from the heat, add 1 cup of crushed peppermint, and stir to dissolve the candy; allow to cool completely. Add the vanilla, sweetened condensed milk, lemon juice, and salt, transfer to a large bowl, and set aside in the refrigerator.

2. In a separate bowl whip the heavy cream until it reaches soft peak. Fold the cream gently into the peppermint mixture, then transfer one-third of the mixture to a shallow freezable container. Sprinkle on one-third of the remaining peppermints, and repeat with the remaining mixtures. The ice cream will swirl itself when you scoop it.

3. Cover with plastic wrap or waxed paper pressed directly on the surface of the ice cream, and place it in the freezer for 6 hours.

4. Scoop and serve with whipped cream, hot fudge sauce, white chocolate sauce, or fresh strawberries.

meyer lemon ice cream

MAKES ABOUT 1 QUART OF ICE CREAM

Yes, lemon is a bright, sunshiny flavor (think lemonade), but its season is actually winter. The Meyer lemon grows like a weed in Southern California. Just about everyone has one in the back-yard (or in their neighbor's yard, within reach). Their flavor is more subtle than the typical grocery store lemon, a bit milder, and a bit less acidic. They are available in the markets during the winter, but if you can't find them, any old lemon will do. See page 151 for an additional Variation.

INGREDIENTS

¾ cup fresh Meyer lemon juice

Finely grated zest of 2 lemons

Pinch of salt

One 13-ounce can sweetened condensed milk

1 cup milk

2 cups heavy cream

METHOD

1. In a large bowl, combine the lemon juice, zest, salt, and sweetened condensed milk. Slowly stir in the milk.

2. In a separate bowl, whip the heavy cream until it reaches soft peak. Fold the cream into the lemon base, then transfer the mixture to a shallow freezable container.

3. Cover with plastic wrap or waxed paper pressed directly on the surface of the ice cream, and place it in the freezer for 6 hours.

4. Scoop and serve with extra dark chocolate sauce, chocolate sorbet, lavender granita, sweetened whipped cream, fresh berry salsa, or thyme shortbread.

VARIATIONS

LEMON-THYME: A lovely pair, lemon and thyme brighten the winter with the essence of a spring garden. Strip the fresh thyme leaves off their stem and crush them a little with a quick chop of a knife to release their oils. Add them to the mixture before the whipped cream is folded in.

RUBY RED GRAPEFRUIT: This is an underappreciated fruit, and one that I think deserves a better spot on the menu than halved on the breakfast table. Use grapefruit juice in place of the lemon juice, but don't use the bitter grapefruit zest. A combination of lemon and orange zests works better. Serve it with citrus salsa and a quick grind of pink peppercorns.

Meyer Lemon Ice Cream

pumpkin ice cream

MAKES ABOUT 1 QUART OF ICE CREAM

Often considered the property of Thanksgiving, the pumpkin rightly belongs to all of the cold months. Here, though, as tradition dictates, it is paired with a standard spice mix. See the Variations for some new interpretations. See page 151 for more Variations.

INGREDIENTS

1½ cups pumpkin puree

One 13-ounce can sweetened condensed milk

1 cup milk

¼ teaspoon freshly grated nutmeg

1 teaspoon ground cardamom

1/8 teaspoon ground cinnamon

1/8 teaspoon ground allspice

A tiny pinch of ground cloves

½ teaspoon salt

2 cups heavy cream

METHOD

1. In a large bowl, combine the pumpkin puree, sweetened condensed milk, milk, spices, and salt.

2. In a separate bowl, whip the heavy cream until it reaches soft peak. Fold the cream gently into pumpkin mixture, then transfer to a shallow freezable container.

3. Cover with plastic wrap or waxed paper directly on the surface of the ice cream, and place it in the freezer for 6 hours.

4. Scoop and serve with caramel sauce, dried fruit compote, toasted pumpkin-seed brittle, or whipped cream, and a grating of nutmeg.

VARIATION

PUMPKIN, ROSEMARY, AND RAISIN: Soak 1 cup of mixed golden and black raisins in boiling water until they are plumped, about 15 minutes. Chop 1 tablespoon of fresh rosemary needles very finely (I like to run them through my coffee mill). Drain the liquid from the plumped raisins. Omit the spices from the main recipe, and add the rosemary and raisins to the pumpkin base before the cream is folded in. Then proceed with the recipe as directed.

PUMPKIN PUREE

Pumpkin puree is easy enough to find in the market, but if you are interested in using up that jack-o-lantern, or you have some interesting squash on hand, why not make your own? There are a few methods that you can choose from. Peeled and diced, they can be tossed lightly in oil and spread out on a baking sheet, or boiled or steamed until tender. The boiled and steamed versions will take on a little extra liquid, so be prepared for that in your recipe. Smaller squash can be sliced in half, seeded, roasted, and then, when cooled, scooped from the skin.

Pumpkin, Rosemary, and
Raisin Ice Cream with
Winter Fruit Compote
(recipe on page 142)

apple-spice ice cream

MAKES ABOUT 1 QUART OF ICE CREAM

I love apples in the winter. The best varieties come out then, and it just seems overall like a winter flavor. Apple pie, apple dumplings, hot apple cider, all evoke the need to snuggle down and stay warm. (Yes, even in Southern California.) This recipe evokes the best of that feeling. Fuji apples are my default variety for this recipe, but I'll pick whatever variety comes to the farmers' market for a limited time in the fall. You should choose whichever apple tastes the best to you.

INGREDIENTS

¼ cup apple cider vinegar

4 cups peeled, cored, and sliced apples

1 fat slice lemon rind

1 cinnamon stick, crushed (Mexican cinnamon preferred)

1 whole clove

1 piece star anise

1 to 2 whole cardamom pods, crushed

1 teaspoon grated peeled fresh ginger

1 cup milk

One 13-ounce can sweetened condensed milk

Pinch of salt

2 cups heavy cream

METHOD

1. Combine the vinegar, apples, lemon rind, and spices in a large saucepan over high heat. Cook, stirring occasionally, until the apples are tender and the liquid has reduced. Remove from the heat and cool completely.

2. Run the apples through a blender to puree, and strain out any large fibers and spice chunks through a fine-mesh strainer. Add the milk, sweetened condensed milk, and salt.

3. In a separate bowl, whip the heavy cream until it reaches soft peak. Fold the cream gently into the apple mixture, then transfer to a shallow freezable container.

4. Cover with plastic wrap or waxed paper pressed directly on the surface of the ice cream, and place it in the freezer for 6 hours.

5. Scoop and serve with caramel sauce, candied pecans, sautéed pumpkin, winter fruit compote, maple sugar glaze, or black walnut pesto. This also makes a terrific float when combined with sparkling cider.

VARIATIONS

CARAMEL-APPLE: Omit the spices and hold off on the vinegar. Cook the apples over high heat in 2 tablespoons of butter and ¼ cup of packed brown sugar, stirring continuously, until they are well caramelized. Add the vinegar and an additional ¼ cup of water to the pan, reduce the heat, and cook until the apples are tender and the liquid has reduced. Replace ¼ cup of the milk with sour cream, then proceed with the recipe as directed.

APPLE-CARAMEL SWIRL: Put an inch of ice cream base in the freezable container, then swirl caramel sauce on top. Repeat with another inch of ice cream, more caramel sauce, etc., until the container is full. Freeze as directed. Don't stir it into a swirl. The ice cream will swirl itself as you scoop.

APPLE-WALNUT CRUNCH: Omit all the spices but the nutmeg. Prepare 2 cups of Brown Sugar–Candied Nuts, page 144, and set them aside to cool completely. Chop the nuts to chocolate-chip size, and fold them into the base with the whipped cream.

APPLE-ROSEMARY: In the olden days I was hired for a pastry chef job based on this recipe. Replace the spices with 2 tablespoons of finely chopped fresh rosemary needles. Serve the finished ice cream with fresh apples sautéed in butter and a tablespoon of sugar until caramelized.

PEAR ICE CREAM: Use this same method with fresh, ripe pears. They will benefit from the same spices, or reduce to just one or two.

Apple-Spice Ice Cream
with Caramel Sauce
(*recipe on page 136*)

cold-weather ice creams •

caramel ice cream

Because caramel is thick and sweet, we can omit the sweetened condensed milk from this recipe. I have added evaporated milk instead, which is the same consistency, but not sweet. You can also use half-and-half or heavy cream, but I find that the added cream makes the end product too fatty on the palate. See page 151 for an additional Variation.

INGREDIENTS

1 cup sugar

¼ cup water

1 teaspoon fresh lemon juice

2 cups evaporated milk

1 tablespoon apple cider vinegar

½ teaspoon kosher salt

2 cups heavy cream

METHOD

1. Combine the sugar and water in a small saucepan. (Choose a pan that seems a bit too big—you'll see why in a minute.) Gently mix the sugar and water together so that it resembles wet sand. Be sure there are no stray grains of sugar on the side of the pan. Wash these down with a wet hand to prevent crystallization. Place the pan on the stovetop over high heat. Do not move the pan around or stir.

2. When the sugar begins to boil, add the lemon juice. Do not stir it in—the bubbles will do the stirring for you. Continue to cook until the mixture turns a dark amber color. This will happen fairly fast, so stay close. When it does, remove the pan from the heat.

3. Immediately whisk in the evaporated milk. The mixture will bubble up and steam like molten lava, so be prepared for that. Some cooks like to wear an oven mitt to protect their hands from the steam. When the milk is well incorporated, add the vinegar and salt. Cool the mixture completely over an ice bath. (See note on Ice Baths, page 62.)

4. In a separate bowl, whip the heavy cream until it reaches soft peak, then gently pour the cooled caramel mixture on top and fold them together. Transfer the mixture to a shallow freezable container.

5. Cover with plastic wrap or waxed paper pressed directly on the surface of the ice cream, and place it in the freezer for 6 hours.

Tangerine-Caramel Ice Cream *(recipe on page 62)*, with candied tangerine zest and Caramel Sauce *(recipes on pages 146 and 136)*

6. Scoop and serve with a dollop of crème fraîche, toasted nuts, sautéed pears, winter fruit compote, or a sprinkle of sea salt.

VARIATIONS

TANGERINE-CARAMEL: For this mouthwatering combination, add the finely grated zest of 4 tangerines and 2 tablespoons of orange liqueur to the caramel base. Serve with a mixture of winter citrus suprêmes. For added zing, this combination pairs well with a little heat from red chile flakes; add ¼ to ½ teaspoon.

CARAMEL–FLEUR DE SEL: Put an inch of your ice cream base in the freezable container, then sprinkle a layer of your finest sea salt on top. Repeat with another inch of ice cream, more sea salt, etc., until the container is full. Freeze as directed. The salt will be more apparent on the palate when sprinkled in this manner, as opposed to stirring it into the base.

TURTLE ICE CREAM: Turtles are delectable caramel-chocolate-pecan candies. Toast 2 cups of chopped pecans until golden brown and fragrant (see page 33). When completely cool, put an inch of ice cream base in the freezable container, then sprinkle on some pecans, and swirl chocolate ganache on top. Repeat with another inch of ice cream, more pecans and ganache, etc., until the container is full. Freeze as directed. Don't stir it into a swirl. The ice cream will swirl itself as you scoop.

CARAMEL AND WINTER FRUITS: Caramel is the perfect counterpoint to rich, sweet, and tangy dried fruits. Make your own 2-cup blend of your favorite dried fruits. Consider apricots, dates, figs, golden raisins, currants, dried cherries, or cranberries. Add the zest of 1 orange and ¼ cup of dark rum or brandy. Cover with boiling water and set aside to plump and cool for at least 30 minutes (ideally overnight). Drain off the liquid before layering the fruit with the caramel ice cream as for a swirl.

ICE BATHS

The fastest way to cool something down is over ice water. You need two containers, one smaller than the other. Fill the large one half full of ice. Fill the smaller one with the mixture to be cooled. Nestle the small container in the ice, then add water to the larger container of ice. Stir the mixture every few minutes for speediest cooling. This is also the safest way to cool anything, taking it out of the food danger zone (40 to 140°F is the ideal temperature for bacteria growth), and faster than any other cooling method.

---

rum-raisin ice cream

MAKES ABOUT 1 QUART OF ICE CREAM

When I was a kid, I loved rum-raisin ice cream. I felt like I was getting away with something. Today, that flavor still makes me feel a little bit naughty, even though I have been of drinking age for many moons. Rum-flavored raisins can be prepared quickly, but if you can plan ahead, they are much better when allowed to macerate overnight.

INGREDIENTS

1 cup golden raisins

1 cup dark raisins

½ cup dried currants

1 cup dark rum (Myers's is the pastry chef's preference)

1 tablespoon pure vanilla extract

One 13-ounce can sweetened condensed milk

1 cup milk

1½ teaspoons fresh lemon juice

¼ teaspoon salt

2 cups heavy cream

METHOD

1. In a small heatproof container combine the golden raisins, dark raisins, currants, rum, and vanilla. Add enough boiling water to cover. Set aside for at least 30 minutes, or overnight if you have time.

2. In a large bowl, combine the sweetened condensed milk, milk, lemon juice, and salt.

3. In a separate bowl, whip the heavy cream until it reaches soft peak. Fold the cream gently into the milk mixture, then transfer one-third of the mixture to a shallow freezable container. Gently drain excess liquid from raisins. (Don't squeeze or press it all out—you want some of that delicious nectar in your ice cream!) Sprinkle on one-third of the soaked raisins. Top with another third of the ice cream mixture, add another third of the raisins, etc. Do not stir the mixture together. The ice cream will swirl itself when you scoop it.

4. Cover with plastic wrap or waxed paper pressed directly on the surface of the ice cream, and place it in the freezer for 6 hours.

5. Scoop and serve with an added sprinkle of macerated raisins, caramel-rum sauce, rum-spiked whipped cream, chopped toasted walnuts, or diced grilled pineapple.

Rum-Raisin Ice Cream sandwiched
on coconut macaroons

VANILLA-RUM-RAISIN: Rum and vanilla are made to be together. While the recipe above calls for vanilla extract, adding a whole split and scraped vanilla bean in its place is really amazing.

COCONUT-RUM-RAISIN: Rum suggests the tropics, which is why substituting unsweetened coconut milk for the regular milk is a delicious idea.

PINEAPPLE-RUM-RAISIN: This is another great tropical combination. Fold in 1 extremely well-drained 8-ounce can of crushed pineapple to the ice cream base before the whipped cream is folded in.

RAISIN VARIETALS

I use a blend of raisins, because that's what I find the most pleasing to the eye and palate. But by all means, use whichever raisin you like. There are some odd ones out there if you know where to look. (Hint: the Internet.) My husband grew up in the Fresno area, in the heart of California's raisin country. As a consequence, I fell in love with both him and the Muscat raisin, something I highly recommend in this and similar recipes if you can find them. (The raisin, I mean—he's taken.)

california date ice cream

I am infatuated with dates. I never had them much as a kid, except in my grandmother's date bars, which I considered old-lady food. But when I began cooking for money, I discovered many fine qualities of the date —they are supersweet without the guilt, chock-full of nutrients and fiber, they add moisture to just about any recipe, and they last seemingly forever. Here, in Southern California, we drive out to the desert for a famous date shake at Hadley's Fruit Orchards. Just one of our many SoCal perks. This recipe is the next best thing.

INGREDIENTS

2 cups pitted dates

Finely grated zest of 1 orange

1 cup milk

One 13-ounce can sweetened condensed milk

1 tablespoon fresh lemon juice

Pinch of salt

2 cups heavy cream

METHOD

1. Combine the dates and zest in a medium bowl. Cover with boiling water, and set aside to soak until completely cool. (Do this a day ahead for best results.)

2. Drain the dates and puree them in a food processor or blender, adding the cup of milk slowly to facilitate blending. Pour the date puree through a fine-mesh strainer to remove the skins.

3. In a large bowl, combine the date puree, sweetened condensed milk, lemon juice, and salt.

4. In a separate bowl, whip the heavy cream until it reaches soft peak. Fold the cream gently into the date mixture, then transfer to a shallow freezable container.

5. Cover with plastic wrap or waxed paper pressed directly on the surface of the ice cream, and place it in the freezer for 6 hours.

6. Scoop and serve with whipped cream, candied walnuts, salted caramel sauce, Bananas Foster, grilled pineapple, or sandwich a scoop between two coconut macaroons.

DATE-PARMESAN: Don't turn up your nose until you've tried it. Super-salty Parmesan cheese makes a lovely balanced partner with supersweet dates. Fold ½ cup of freshly, finely grated Parmesan cheese into the date puree. For best results use the finest Parmigiano Reggiano.

COCONUT-DATE: Since they grow on palm trees, dates are perfectly suited to tropical flavors. Replace the regular milk with canned unsweetened coconut milk. You can even up the coconut ante by using coconut water to plump your dates.

DRIED APRICOT–ALMOND ICE CREAM: Use the same procedure but substitute dried apricots for the dates. Before pouring the boiling water over the fruit, add ¼ cup of amaretto. Serve this version with candied almonds, amaretti cookies, or almond macaroons.

PRUNE-ARMAGNAC: Booze-soaked prunes might sound like a crazy grandma's remedy but, in fact, it is a classic combination from the Armagnac region of France, where the best cognac in the world is made. (And where the happiest grannies reside.) Substitute prunes for the dates, and add ½ cup Armagnac, cognac, or the best brandy you can afford to the fruits before pouring on the hot water. Serve with crisp molasses wafers or gingersnaps.

California Date Ice Cream with
Caramel Sauce, Parmesan Tuiles
(recipes on pages 136 and 148),
and Parmesan-stuffed dates

honey-kumquat ice cream

Kumquats look like tiny little oranges, but they are actually in a different botanical family. Not that it matters when you pop one in your mouth. If you are a fan of marmalade and grapefruit, you'll probably like the kumquat. They are all zest and seed, and very little pulp. Fresh and raw they pack a punch. But simmered and stewed, the citrus oil mellows, and they transform into an exotic treat. See page 152 for Variations.

INGREDIENTS

2 cups fresh kumquats, quartered lengthwise

2 tablespoons honey

Pinch of kosher salt

1 tablespoon lemon juice

1 teaspoon orange flower water or ¼ teaspoon orange extract

1 cup milk

One 13-ounce can sweetened condensed milk

2 cups heavy cream

METHOD

1. Bring a medium saucepan of water to a boil, and add the quartered kumquats. The bubbles will briefly subside, but when they come back up, cook for 1 minute, then strain out the fruit. Repeat this step one more time with a fresh pot of water. It helps leach out the bitterness.

2. Place the twice-blanched-and-drained kumquats back in a clean saucepan, add the honey and an additional ½ cup of water, and simmer again until the liquid has reduced and the kumquats are tender. Cool completely. Loose seeds can be removed, although eating them is part of the kumquat's charm.

3. When completely cool, combine the kumquats, salt, lemon juice, orange flower water, milk, and sweetened condensed milk.

4. In a separate bowl, whip the heavy cream until it reaches soft peak. Fold the cream gently into the kumquat mixture, then transfer to a shallow freezable container.

5. Cover with plastic wrap or waxed paper pressed directly on the surface of the ice cream, and place it in the freezer for 6 hours.

6. Scoop and serve with whipped cream, marmalade sauce, dried fruit compote, citrus salsa, brioche toast, orange-caramel sauce, or gingered poached pears.

Honey-Kumquat Ice Cream

sweet potato–marshmallow swirl ice cream

MAKES ABOUT 1 QUART OF ICE CREAM

This classic combo lends itself perfectly to ice cream. You can use yams or sweet potatoes. They are interchangeable and, in fact, most of the yams we get in the United States are technically sweet potatoes. True yams are much sweeter and starchier, often purple or white, and typically only available in Asian markets. See page 152 for more Variations.

INGREDIENTS

2 cups fresh or canned sweet potato puree

1 tablespoon molasses

¼ teaspoon freshly grated nutmeg

¼ teaspoon ground ginger

¼ teaspoon ground cinnamon

¼ teaspoon ground cardamom

A very small pinch of ground cloves

1 tablespoon fresh lemon juice

Pinch of salt

¾ cup milk

¼ cup sour cream

One 13-ounce can sweetened condensed milk

2 cups heavy cream

1 cup Marshmallow Fluff (aka marshmallow creme)

METHOD

1. In a large bowl, stir together the sweet potato puree, molasses, spices, lemon juice, and salt. Stir in the milk, sour cream, and sweetened condensed milk.

2. In a separate bowl, whip the heavy cream until it reaches soft peak. Fold the cream gently into the sweet potato mixture, then transfer one-third of the mixture to a freezable container. Spread on one-third of the Marshmallow Fluff, top with another third of the ice cream, another third of the fluff, and so on.

3. Cover with plastic wrap or waxed paper pressed directly on the surface of the ice cream, and place in the freezer for 6 hours.

4. Scoop and serve with more fluff, whipped cream, German chocolate topping, toasted pecans, caramel sauce, brandied dried fruit compote, or marmalade sauce. This also makes a cool version of Baked Alaska (see page 125).

PURPLE PERUVIAN POTATO: Potatoes are native to the Andes, where the earliest varieties came in a rainbow of colors. Purple Peruvians are not sweet, but they make a fantastic ice cream. Omit the spices from the above recipe, and add ¼ cup honey. Then proceed with the recipe, minus the fluff swirl. You can also steep 2 tablespoons of lavender in the milk for a delightfully floral variation.

Purple Peruvian Potato Ice Cream

PREPARING SWEET POTATOES

Sweet potatoes are available already cooked in cans, but it is easy (and cheaper) to make your own puree. Wrap three large whole sweet potatoes in aluminum foil and roast until soft (about an hour at 350°F). When cool, peel and mash them. Or you can peel your potatoes, cut them into large chunks, and boil or steam until tender. This is a little quicker, as is tossing them lightly in oil and roasting them in the oven. Each will yield a slightly different product. Keep in mind that boiled or steamed potatoes will have more water in them. When you are not up to any of these options, you can buy a can already pureed. (Or try my secret in-a-hurry weapon, baby food!)

moon pie ice cream

I have been obsessed with the Moon Pie ever since I was handed an assortment at a food show several years ago. In my eyes, they are the quintessential American flavor, because they taste like childhood, and therefore hope. The combination is strikingly similar to the S'more, which makes sense, because they are both wonderful.

INGREDIENTS

1 cup chocolate chips

1 cup milk

1 teaspoon pure vanilla extract

One 13-ounce can sweetened condensed milk

1 tablespoon unsweetened cocoa powder

1 tablespoon fresh lemon juice

Pinch of salt

2 cups heavy cream

1 cup Marshmallow Fluff (aka marshmallow creme)

1 cup graham crackers, roughly crumbled

METHOD

1. Microwave the chocolate in 15-second increments, stirring in between, until completely melted.

2. In a large bowl, combine the chocolate, milk, vanilla, sweetened condensed milk, cocoa powder, lemon juice, and salt. If the mixture is warm, set it aside to cool completely.

3. In a separate bowl, whip the heavy cream until it reaches soft peak. Fold the cream gently into the cooled chocolate milk mixture. Transfer one-third of the mixture to a shallow freezable container. Spread on a third of the Marshmallow Fluff, sprinkle on one-third of the crushed graham crackers, and repeat to fill the container. Don't stir in a swirl. The ice cream will swirl itself when you scoop it.

4. Cover with plastic wrap or waxed paper pressed directly on the surface of the ice cream, and place it in the freezer for 6 hours.

5. Scoop and serve with whipped cream, shaved chocolate, sautéed bananas, or top with more fluff and toast it with a propane torch. (You have one of those, right?)

VARIATIONS

BANANA–MOON PIE: One of the most delicious Moon Pie flavors is banana. Make it your own by layering slices of sweet ripe bananas with the fluff and grahams in the above recipe.

CINNAMON-MOON PIE: Omit the melted chocolate chips, and add into the base ½ teaspoon of ground cinnamon. Proceed with the recipe as directed, and swirl in ½ cup of ganache with the fluff and grahams.

PEANUT BUTTER-MOON PIE: Omit the melted chocolate chips, and add ½ cup of peanut butter to the base. Proceed with the recipe as directed, and swirl in ½ cup of ganache with the fluff and grahams.

cardamom ice cream

Although this spice is common year-round in everything from curries to breakfast pastry, for me it is winter on a spoon. That's because every Christmas my grandmother made a Norwegian sugar cookie, exploding with the flavor of cardamom. See page 152 for more Variations.

INGREDIENTS

1 cup milk

2 tablespoons fresh cardamom pods, crushed, or 1 tablespoon ground

1 tablespoon pure vanilla extract

One 13-ounce can sweetened condensed milk

1 tablespoon fresh lemon juice

Pinch of salt

2 cups heavy cream

METHOD

1. Combine the milk, cardamom and vanilla in a small saucepan and bring it to a boil. When it is at the boil, remove from the heat and set aside to steep and cool completely.

2. In a large bowl, combine the cardamom milk, sweetened condensed milk, lemon juice, and salt.

3. Whip heavy cream until it reaches soft peak. Fold the cream gently into the cardamom mixture, then transfer to a shallow freezable container.

4. Cover with plastic wrap or waxed paper pressed directly on the surface of the ice cream, and place it in the freezer for 6 hours.

5. Scoop and serve with whipped cream, dried fruit compote, caramel sauce, sautéed bananas, or gingersnaps.

VARIATION

CHOCOLATE-CARDAMOM: This great combo helped me win $10,000 on Food Network's now-defunct *Sweet Genius* food competition. Microwave 1 cup of chocolate in 15-second increments, stirring in between, until completely melted. Slowly stir in the steeped cardamom milk, then proceed with the recipe as directed.

Chocolate-Cardamom Ice Cream with Winter Fruit Compote and Candied Walnuts *(recipes on pages 142 and 144)*

hazelnut ice cream

MAKES ABOUT 1 QUART OF ICE CREAM

Also known as the filbert, the hazelnut is a classic pastry chef ingredient. Chefs can buy hazelnuts in paste form, but it's hard to use, and even harder for the home cook to find. It's easier, and better, to make your own. See page 152 for Variations.

INGREDIENTS

3 cups hazelnuts

1 cup milk

One 13-ounce can sweetened condensed milk

1 tablespoon pure vanilla extract

1 tablespoon fresh lemon juice

Pinch of salt

2 cups heavy cream

METHOD

1. Preheat the oven to 350°F. Spread the nuts out on a rimmed baking sheet and roast until golden brown and fragrant.

2. Transfer the hot nuts to the bowl of a food processor and grind to a fine powder. Add the milk slowly to create a smooth nut butter.

3. In a large bowl, combine the nut butter, sweetened condensed milk, vanilla, lemon juice, and salt.

4. In a separate bowl, whip the heavy cream until it reaches soft peak. Fold the cream gently into the hazelnut mixture, then transfer to a shallow freezable container.

5. Cover with plastic wrap or waxed paper pressed directly on the surface of the ice cream, and place it in the freezer for 6 hours.

6. Scoop and serve with whipped cream, caramel sauce, cranberry compote, pomegranate glaze, hazelnut brittle, or a shot of Frangelico.

REMOVING THE SKINS FROM HAZELNUTS

If you can find hazelnuts already skinned, choose those. If not, you'll need to remove the skins before processing. It's not hard, but requires an extra step. After the nuts finish toasting, rub them over a mesh strainer, or between two terrycloth towels. The papery skin will flake off, and the nuts can then be separated and used as needed. If you skip this step, that papery skin will really be unpleasantly noticeable in your recipes.

gelatos

~~~~~~

This Italian-style of ice cream is distinguished by the way it is churned. Gelato machines turn slower, and therefore incorporate less air than American ice cream machines. Although this book takes a firm antichurn stance, we can still simulate traditional gelato by slightly thickening the custard base with evaporated milk instead of regular milk, while at the same time using the traditional Italian flavors.

espresso gelato

MAKES ABOUT 1 QUART OF GELATO

In my opinion there is nothing on earth better than a good espresso ice cream. They do it best in Italy, where the gelato is intensely flavored and slowly churned. To approximate this experience, I prefer to use real coffee beans rather than espresso powder or extract. The flavor is richer be-cause the oil of the bean is still present. If you are concerned about falling asleep, go ahead and choose decaffeinated beans. The drip grind is preferable, as the larger bits are easier to strain away, although you will still have some tiny flakes of coffee bean, which are, frankly, delightful.

INGREDIENTS

¼ cup Italian espresso beans, ground for drip (or 3 tablespoons instant espresso powder or coffee extract)

1 cup evaporated milk

3 tablespoons coffee liqueur (see page 80)

1 teaspoon pure vanilla extract

1 tablespoon fresh lemon juice

Pinch of salt

One 13-ounce can sweetened condensed milk

2 cups heavy cream

METHOD

1. Combine the ground espresso beans and the evaporated milk in a small saucepan, bring just to a boil, then set aside to steep and cool completely. Strain through a very fine–mesh strainer, or multiple layers of cheesecloth, to remove the coffee grounds.

2. In a large bowl, combine the coffee milk with the liqueur, vanilla, lemon juice, salt, and sweetened condensed milk.

3. In a separate bowl, whip the heavy cream until it reaches soft peak. Fold the cream gently into the coffee base, then transfer the mixture to a shallow freezable container.

4. Cover with plastic wrap or waxed paper pressed directly on the surface of the ice cream, and place in the freezer for 6 hours.

5. Scoop and serve with chocolate sauce, caramel sauce, a drizzle of coffee liqueur, chocolate-covered espresso beans, crushed almond toffee, or a simple dollop of whipped cream and a shake of cinnamon, like a cappuccino.

VARIATIONS

CINNAMON-COFFEE: This is another typical coffeehouse combination. Add 1 teaspoon of cinnamon to the milk just after it is warmed, then proceed with the recipe as directed.

Espresso Gelato with blondie bars

FLAVORED COFFEE: I am not a huge fan of flavored coffee, but if you are, think about adding one of those Italian coffee syrups to your espresso base instead of the coffee liqueur. Hazelnut, vanilla, caramel—whatever you like in your latte will work here!

MOCHA: Chocolate and coffee are a classic pair for a reason. Create it by adding 2 tablespoons of cocoa powder to the milk just after it is warmed, then proceed with the recipe as directed. Alternatively, layer the ice cream base with chocolate ganache as it is packed for the freezer.

COFFEE-ORANGE: One of my favorites. Add the finely grated zest of 2 oranges to the base before the whipped cream is folded in. Serve this with whipped cream and a candied orange peel garnish. Yum.

COFFEE LIQUEUR

Coffee liqueurs are a dime a dozen. Just about every culture has some variation of it. We are accustomed to Kahlúa in the United States because they advertise the most. But if you have a large liquor mart in your town, investigate some coffee liqueur alternatives. Better yet, make your own. There are two ways to do it—the quick way, and the better way. (Both are still better than store bought, because they are handcrafted with love.) For the quick version: Combine 3 cups of your favorite coffee (prepared and hot) with 1½ cups of packed brown sugar, 3 tablespoons of pure vanilla extract, and 2 cups of vodka. Mix until sugar has dissolved, and cool.

For the better version, you need to work 3 weeks in advance:

Combine in an extra-large glass or ceramic sealable container one 750 ml bottle of clear rum, 2 cups of dark rum (such as Myers's), 1½ cups of sugar, 1 split vanilla bean (pod and all), 1 Mexican cinnamon stick, slightly crushed, 2 cups of whole dark roast coffee beans, and 2 tablespoons of coffee nibs. Stir thoroughly and set in a cool, dark place for 3 weeks. Strain off the liquid into clean canning jars or bottles.

gianduja gelato
(milk chocolate with hazelnut)

Gianduja (zhee-an-doo-yuh) is an Italian hazelnut milk chocolate. It is similar to Nutella in flavor (not coincidentally, another Italian product). But while Nutella is hazelnut butter flavored with cocoa powder, gianduja is actually a milk chocolate, made richer and more chocolaty with the use of cocoa butter, and with a flavor additive of hazelnuts. Gianduja hasn't ever caught on as much in the United States as it has in Europe, but given the popularity of Nutella, it's probably only a matter of time. Your best chance of finding it is in a market that carries lots of international products. American companies make it, too, but it is Italian through and through. See pages 152–53 for Variations.

INGREDIENTS

12 ounces gianduja, finely chopped

1 cup evaporated milk

3 tablespoons Frangelico

1 teaspoon pure vanilla extract

1 tablespoon fresh lemon juice

Pinch of salt

One 13-ounce can sweetened condensed milk

2 cups heavy cream

METHOD

1. Place the chopped gianduja in a large bowl. In a saucepan bring the evaporated milk to a near boil, then pour it over the chopped chocolate. Let sit for 5 minutes, then stir until smooth.

2. Add the liqueur, vanilla, lemon juice, salt, and sweetened condensed milk. If the mixture is still warm, set it aside to cool completely.

3. In a separate bowl, whip the heavy cream until it reaches soft peak. Fold the cream gently into the gianduja base, and transfer the mixture to a shallow freezable container.

4. Cover with plastic wrap or waxed paper pressed directly on the surface of the ice cream, and place in the freezer for 6 hours.

5. Scoop and serve with biscotti, whipped cream, caramel sauce, chopped hazelnuts, Bananas Foster, or a shot of Frangelico.

cioccolato gelato
(chocolate)

MAKES ABOUT 1 QUART OF GELATO

Italian chocolate ice cream has a tendency to be darker than the typical American version. To approximate this, we use unsweetened chocolate. The condensed milk adds enough sugar to approximate the extra-bitter Italian style. If you anticipate an inability to appreciate such a bitter taste, feel free to use a bittersweet chocolate. Or, if you are really into dark chocolate, shoot for a blend of 97% to 99% cocoa solids. The coffee extract is added, not to give a coffee flavor, but to enhance the bitterness.

INGREDIENTS

6 ounces unsweetened chocolate, finely chopped (about 1 cup)

1 teaspoon instant coffee or espresso powder

1 cup evaporated milk

1 teaspoon pure vanilla extract

1½ teaspoons fresh lemon juice

Pinch of salt

One 13-ounce can sweetened condensed milk

2 cups heavy cream

METHOD

1. Combine the chopped unsweetened chocolate and instant espresso powder in a large bowl. In a saucepan bring the evaporated milk to a near boil, then pour it over the chopped chocolate. Let sit for 5 minutes, then stir until smooth.

2. Stir the vanilla, lemon juice, salt, and sweetened condensed milk into the chocolate mixture. If the mixture is still warm, set it aside to cool completely.

3. In a separate bowl, whip the heavy cream until it reaches soft peak. Fold the cream gently into the chocolate mixture and transfer to a shallow freezable container.

4. Cover with plastic wrap or waxed paper pressed directly on the surface of the ice cream, and place in the freezer for 6 hours.

5. Scoop and serve with whipped cream, fresh raspberries, vanilla custard, nut lace cookies, a shot of espresso, or on a bed of orange granita.

LESS BITTER: If you can't fathom cooking with unsweetened chocolate, go ahead and use the bittersweet or semisweet stuff. You can also omit the instant espresso powder if you want to.

MORE BITTER: Really? Well, find some really high-quality 99% cocoa solid chocolate. Not all chocolates are the same, and the manufacturer really does matter. I have favorites, but it's a highly personal preference. Do some chocolate tasting. Visit a chocolatier. Make it a party! Then stock up.

NIBS: Going for a total chocolate experience? Then fold in 1 cup of cocoa nibs with the whipped cream.

mandorla gelato (almond)

MAKES ABOUT 1 QUART OF GELATO

Italy loves its almonds, and what's not to love? They are a huge producer, and they make some of the world's best almond products, including amaretto liqueur, amaretti cookies, and the greatest marzipan on the planet. But, just to be clear, I am a strict California almond user. Also, as you will see in the following recipe, I typically avoid almond extract, because it tastes very artificial to me. You may feel like this is a lot of trouble to go to when you can simply buy almond milk. You're right, except that almond milk doesn't taste toasty enough for me.

INGREDIENTS

2 cups sliced almonds, roughly crushed

2 cups evaporated milk

¼ vanilla bean pod, split and scraped

Finely grated zest of 1 lemon

1 tablespoon fresh lemon juice

Pinch of salt

One 13-ounce can sweetened condensed milk

2 cups heavy cream

METHOD

1. Preheat the oven to 375°F. Spread the almonds out on a rimmed baking sheet and toast them until they are dark and fragrant. Meanwhile, in a large saucepan bring the evaporated milk to a near boil. Off the heat, add the hot toasted nuts to the evaporated milk, stir, and set aside to steep and cool.

2. When completely cool, transfer the nut milk to a blender and puree, then strain the liquid from the nuts, being sure to press out all the liquid. Squeeze and wring out the nuts in a cheesecloth or a thin linen towel to extract as much toasty nutty flavor as possible.

3. In a large bowl, combine the almond milk, vanilla bean, lemon zest, lemon juice, salt, and sweetened condensed milk. If the mixture is still warm, set it aside to cool completely.

4. In a separate bowl, whip the heavy cream until it reaches soft peak. Fold the cream into the almond mixture and transfer to a shallow freezable container.

5. Cover with plastic wrap or waxed paper pressed directly on the surface of the ice cream, and place in the freezer for 6 hours.

6. Scoop and serve with fresh stone fruits (apricots, peaches, plums, cherries), orange suprêmes, caramel sauce, hot fudge sauce, crushed toffee, or a shot of amaretto.

Mandorla
Gelato

VARIATIONS

ALMOND TOFFEE CRUNCH: Before the whipped cream is added, fold in bits of candied almond brittle, almond toffee, or coffee honeycomb candy for a rich, decadent crunch.

MARZIPAN: Fold in pea-size chunks of marzipan. Roll the marzipan into long thin snakes and cut to size using a cornstarch- or powdered sugar–coated knife.

lampone gelato
(raspberry)

For the best raspberry ice cream, choose the finest berries at the peak of ripeness. If, however, you are like me and can rarely find such a thing, consider the frozen berry. They are typically picked at the perfect ripeness and flash-frozen in the field, so the quality is high, and the flavor is dependable. Since the grocer doesn't take kindly to me testing the berries before I buy them, I generally choose the frozen berry first. Occasionally, though, I hit a farmers' market with some incredible products, in which case, I stock up and freeze my own.

INGREDIENTS

2 pints (4 cups) fresh or frozen raspberries

Finely grated zest of 1 lemon

2 tablespoons fresh lemon juice

¼ cup water

Pinch of salt

½ teaspoon pure vanilla extract

1 cup evaporated milk

One 13-ounce can sweetened condensed milk

2 cups heavy cream

METHOD

1. In a large sauté pan, combine the berries, lemon zest, lemon juice, water, and salt. Place over high heat and cook, stirring, until the liquid from the berries exudes. Reduce the heat to medium and cook until the liquid has evaporated and the fruit has taken on a jammy consistency. Remove from the heat and cool completely.

2. In a large bowl, combine raspberry jam, vanilla, evaporated milk, and sweetened condensed milk. If you prefer to remove the raspberry seeds, pass the mixture through a fine-mesh strainer.

3. In a separate bowl, whip the heavy cream until it reaches soft peak. Fold the cream gently into the raspberry base and transfer the mixture to a shallow freezable container.

4. Cover with plastic wrap or waxed paper pressed directly on the surface of the ice cream, and place in the freezer for 6 hours.

5. Scoop and serve with extra dark chocolate sauce, balsamic-caramel sauce, berry-basil compote, crushed hazelnut praline, a dollop of crème fraîche, or a shot of Chambord.

A BERRY OF A DIFFERENT COLOR: Blackberries, boysenberries, blueberries, olalliberries, marionberries, and huckleberries are all great choices for this recipe. If it's purple or red, there's a good bet it will make a fantastic ice cream. And don't forget golden raspberries! And fraises de bois! These tiny wild strawberries have a distinctive flavor that is positively addictive. Whenever you come across delicious interesting berries, try them in this recipe.

CHOCOLATE SWIRL: Chocolate and raspberries are an overused combination, to be sure. But there is a reason everyone likes it. Layer chocolate ganache with this raspberry ice cream as it is packed for the freezer for a different twist on this classic pair.

HERB-INFUSED: Berries, like lemons, take kindly to herbs. Try infusing Thai basil, opal basil, thyme, or sage in this recipe. Combine ¼ cup of the finely chopped herb with the evaporated milk in a small saucepan and bring it to a boil. Remove from the heat, cool completely, then proceed with the recipe as directed. You can strain out the herbs if you like, or leave them in for effect.

SPICE IT UP: Heat and sweet acidity work wonders on the tongue. Try adding a teaspoon of coarsely ground black or pink peppercorns to the base before the whipped cream is folded in. Or make it exotic by steeping 1 teaspoon of crushed cardamom pods or toasted anise seeds in the evaporated milk, as described above for herbs.

Lampone Gelato

fior di latte gelato
(flower of milk, or sweet cream)

MAKES ABOUT 1 QUART OF GELATO

This is Italy's answer to plain vanilla, but it's far from plain. The honey adds a delightful acidity that makes it the perfect platform on which to build a dessert. Be sure to try the affogato variation below, an Italian standard.

INGREDIENTS

1 cup evaporated milk

2 tablespoons honey

1 teaspoon pure vanilla extract

1 tablespoon fresh lemon juice

Pinch of salt

One 13-ounce can sweetened condensed milk

2 cups heavy cream

METHOD

1. In a small microwave-safe bowl or measuring cup, combine the evaporated milk with the honey and warm in the microwave for 30 to 60 seconds to dissolve the honey. Set aside to cool.

2. In a large bowl, combine the honey milk, vanilla, lemon juice, salt, and sweetened condensed milk.

3. In a separate bowl, whip the heavy cream until it reaches soft peak. Fold the cream gently into the honey mixture and transfer to a shallow freezable container.

4. Cover with plastic wrap or waxed paper pressed directly on the surface of the ice cream, and freeze for 6 hours.

5. Scoop and serve with whipped cream, fresh berries, dried fruit compote, amaretti cookies, chocolate sauce, or a shot of dark rum.

VARIATIONS

AFFOGATO: This is simply Fior di Latte topped with a shot of hot espresso and a dollop of whipped cream. To. Die. For.

STRACCIATELLA: This is the classy Italian version of chocolate chip ice cream. It is nothing more than Fior di Latte with chocolate bits. I prefer hand chopping a bittersweet chocolate bar, but store-bought mini chocolate chips are perfectly acceptable. Fold them in with the whipped cream.

sorbets

~~~~~~

In the United States, we are most familiar with the sweet sorbets, enjoyed as a light dessert, or as a refreshing treat on a seaside vacation. But sorbet has a place at the dinner table, too. In some very fine dining establishments you can still find the tradition of a savory sorbet served as a palate cleanser. It is an old idea that is much appreciated by chefs. Sorbets give the mouth a break between very rich or flavorful dishes, allowing you to fully appreciate the artistry of every course. I love this tradition, and I also love the idea of savory sorbets in a full course of their own. Consider a mixed baby green salad topped with a cool herbaceous sorbet dressing, a gazpacho float with golden tomato–cucumber sorbet, or cilantro-avocado-lime sorbet with a ceviche topping. The possibilities are endless.

A NOTE ON SORBET

A classic sorbet is nothing but a frozen fruit puree. There is no custard, eggs, or dairy—just fruit and some portion of sugar. The liquefied fruit, made thick by its pulp, creates a "creamy-ish" texture when frozen. Thinner liquids with no pulp need the addition of a thick syrup, known in the business as "simple syrup," to create the right texture when frozen.

Simple syrup has long been a best friend to pastry chefs and bartenders. It is used not only to give viscosity to sorbet, but also to add moisture to layer cakes, lend a sweet base to dessert sauces, and to sweeten cocktails, iced teas, and lemonades.

The basic recipe is equal parts sugar and water, brought just to the boil. Some recipes increase or decrease the sugar to suit the application. Consider making a bigger batch, and keeping it on hand for some culinary experimentation. If you have simple syrup lying around, whipping up sorbet is even easier—if that's possible. (You'll find a full recipe on pages 137–38.)

Sorbet recipes freeze faster than the ice creams, but they require attention during the freeze. Repeated stirring breaks up the ice crystals as they form and keeps the mix from becoming a solid block of ice. The sorbet is at its very best at the 4-hour mark. If left in the freezer for an extended period without stirring, it will freeze solid, and require a warm-up and re-stir.

Finally, recipes with fruit are notoriously under- or oversweetened. This is because every variety, crop, grower, and season produces fruits with different levels of sweetness. Use these recipes as a guide, but use your own taste buds, too. Add sweetness with more simple syrup, or reduce it with lemon juice. And don't forget the salt, which, when used sparingly, will perk up the blandest of fruits.

BLENDERS, PROCESSORS AND STRAINERS

For fine purees, the blender is king. Its narrow cavity forces the food into the blade for fast, repeated grinding. A food processor will work, too, but not as well. The centrifugal force sends the food to the side of the bowl, away from the blade. In the food processor fine purees are only possible with a very full bowl, or by repeatedly scraping down the sides. It is also possible to make puree without a machine. In the olden days, soft foods were simply pushed through a strainer, which is what you should do if you do not possess a blender or food processor. Think of it as honoring your ancestors.

Midway through stirring
Chocolate Sorbet

tomato-cucumber sorbet

MAKES ABOUT 1 QUART OF SORBET

This makes a fantastic palate cleanser, or you can spike up the spice and serve it as an alternative to gazpacho. See Variation below and an additional Variation on page 153.

INGREDIENTS

8 fresh or canned ripe plum (Roma) tomatoes, halved

1 large cucumber, peeled and cut into chunks

½ cup fresh cilantro leaves, chopped

Juice and zest of 1 lime

1 tablespoon sugar

Pinch of salt

METHOD

1. Combine the tomatoes, cucumbers, and cilantro in the bowl of a food processor or bar blender and process until smooth, adding cold water slowly, as needed, to facilitate the blending. Add the lime zest and juice, sugar, and salt, then adjust the seasoning as necessary.

2. Pass the mixture through a fine-mesh strainer into a shallow freezable container. Cover loosely with plastic or waxed paper and place in the freezer. Stir every 30 minutes until it starts to hold its shape. In about 4 hours it will have attained a scoopable consistency.

3. Scoop into chilled glasses or bowls. As a palate cleanser, serve with a sprig of cilantro. As an appetizer, use it to top a fresh cucumber, radish, and onion salad.

VARIATION

GAZPACHO SORBET: This is the same basic idea, but much more flavorful, because it is not intended to cleanse the palate, but to excite it. Omit the sugar from the above recipe and add to the blender a full cup of fresh cilantro, 2 chopped scallions, 1 roasted Anaheim or poblano chile, and ¼ teaspoon of ground cumin.

Gazpacho Sorbet

raspberry–opal basil sorbet

MAKES ABOUT 1 QUART OF SORBET

Raspberry sorbet is just fine by itself, but I love the addition of opal basil. It is a little less grassy than traditional basil, a little more floral, and a little more "anise-y." Thai basil is very similar, although it lacks the purple hue of the opal variety. If, however, you don't want to appear culinarily snooty, or you just like your raspberries plain, feel free to omit the basil altogether. Or, if you want to fall somewhere in between, use standard basil. (Sometimes it's better to ease into "snoot-itude.")

INGREDIENTS

1 cup sugar

1 cup water

½ cup fresh opal basil leaves
(or regular or Thai basil)

Zest of ½ lemon

4 cups fresh raspberries

Juice of ½ lemon

Pinch of salt

METHOD

1. Combine the sugar and water in a small saucepan and bring to a boil over high heat. Remove from the heat, and let steep and cool completely. Strain out the basil leaves and discard.

2. Place the raspberries and lemon zest into the bowl of a bar blender or food processor and process the berries until chunky. Slowly add the simple syrup and continue to puree until smooth. Pass the mixture through a fine-mesh strainer to remove unwanted seeds. Season with lemon juice and salt, as needed, then transfer the mixture to a shallow freezable container.

3. Cover loosely with plastic or waxed paper and place in the freezer. Stir the mix every 30 minutes until it starts to hold its shape. In about 4 hours it will have attained a scoopable consistency.

4. Scoop into chilled glasses or bowls with fresh berries, crème fraîche or sour cream, madeleines, almond tuile cigarettes, or a splash of champagne.

VARIATIONS

BERRIATIONS: Try this recipe with other great berries. Basil complements black, blue, and huckleberries just as nicely. There are some wonderful varieties around the country, especially in the summer. When you find a delicious berry that is only available for

Raspberry–Opal Basil
Sorbet sandwiched in
chocolate cookies

a limited time, consider purchasing a larger quantity, and freezing some for later. (Olalliberry sorbet makes a great accompaniment to a caramel-pumpkin cake in the fall.) Wash, dry, pack in ziptop plastic bags, and keep them in the freezer for up to 6 months.

GOLDEN RASPBERRY: These gems taste like a red raspberry, but they are yellow! It always makes for a surprising bite. It also makes a beautiful swirl. Make two batches of raspberry sorbet, one yellow and one red. When they are both scoopable, layer them together in a new freezer container, and freeze together, unstirred, for another hour. They will swirl together as they are scooped.

ANOTHER HERB: The raspberry is very accepting of flavors. Try a different herb, such as thyme, bay leaf, chervil, or tarragon. Pair it with a single spice, like ginger (fresh or dried), anise (seed or star), toasted coriander seed, or peppercorns. You can also experiment with vinegars (balsamic, champagne, malt), sugars (brown, maple, date), condiments (mustard, horseradish, wasabi) and salts (sel gris, Maldon, smoked). The greatest dishes I ever made started with me just fooling around like this.

quince sorbet

MAKES ABOUT 1 QUART OF SORBET

Quince is a seasonal product, available in the late summer and fall. It is not a hugely popular fruit in the United States because it can't be eaten out of hand. It needs loving preparation. When carefully poached, it takes on a beautiful pink hue and a delicate floral flavor that will make you a quince convert. See page 153 for Variations.

INGREDIENTS

4 large quince, peeled, seeded, and cut into large chunks (about 2 pounds)

4 cups water

½ cup sugar

¼ cup honey

Finely grated zest of ½ lemon

¼ vanilla bean, split and scraped

Juice of ½ lemon

Pinch of salt

METHOD

1. Combine the quince chunks in a large saucepan with the water, sugar, honey, lemon zest, and vanilla bean and bring to a boil over high heat. Reduce to a simmer, cover partially, and cook until tender, 40 to 50 minutes.

2. Drain the tender quince, reserving the poaching liquid, and cool both completely.

3. Place the cooked and drained quince in the bowl of a bar blender or food processor and process until chunky. Slowly add the poaching syrup, and continue processing, adding only as much syrup as is necessary to achieve a smooth puree. Pass the mixture through a fine-mesh strainer to remove unwanted fibers and vanilla bean. Season with lemon juice and salt, then transfer the mixture to a shallow freezable container.

4. Cover loosely with plastic or waxed paper and place in the freezer. Stir the mixture every 30 minutes until it starts to hold its shape. In about 4 hours it will have attained a scoopable consistency.

5. Scoop into chilled glasses or bowls and serve with whipped cream, rose-caramel glaze, winter fruit compote, candied walnuts, reduced mulled wine sauce, gingersnaps, almond biscotti, toasted brioche, or fruitcake.

mango sorbet

MAKES ABOUT 1 QUART OF SORBET

Mango sorbet seems to be in every grocery store freezer section. But the mangos are in the store, too, and if you could make a fresh, homemade version without additives or preservatives, and be able to adjust the seasoning according to your taste, why wouldn't you? You would! Right? See Variations on page 153.

INGREDIENTS

1 cup sugar

1 cup water

4 large ripe mangos, peeled, pitted, and cut into large chunks

Finely grated zest and juice of 1 small lime

Pinch of salt

METHOD

1. Combine the sugar and water in a small saucepan and bring to a boil over high heat to create a simple syrup. Remove from the heat, and let cool completely.

2. Place the mangos in the bowl of a food processor or bar blender and process until smooth, adding the simple syrup slowly, as needed, to facilitate the blending. Season with lime zest and juice and salt, then transfer the mixture to a shallow freezable container.

3. Cover loosely with plastic or waxed paper and place in the freezer. Stir the mixture every 30 minutes until it starts to hold its shape. In about 4 hours it will have attained a scoopable consistency.

4. Scoop into chilled glasses or bowls and serve with fresh berries, ginger whipped cream, lime curd, cajeta caramel sauce, rose-scented shortbread, coconut rice pudding, coconut macaroons, chopped toasted macadamia nuts, or rum cake.

PEELING AND DICING A MANGO

The easiest way to get at the mango meat is to put away the peeler, and grab a big serving spoon and a knife. Pick ripe mangos that are soft to the touch, then cut them in half along each flat side of the pit. Use the big spoon to scoop out the flesh, as you would an avocado. Then dice as needed. You can cut off a little extra meat from the edge of the pit, or save that for "chef's snack."

poached pear sorbet

MAKES ABOUT 1 QUART OF SORBET

The flavor of a pear sorbet can stay as natural as you'd like, or it can be augmented by way of the poaching liquid. If you are interested in a pure pear flavor, keep the liquid neutral by using only water. If you'd like a more seasonal, spiced-up pear flavor, use wine and spices. See pages 153–54 for Variations.

INGREDIENTS

6 large pears, peeled, seeded, and cut into large chunks

4 cups water

1 cup sugar

Finely grated zest of ½ lemon

Juice of ½ lemon

Pinch of salt

METHOD

1. Combine the pears in a large saucepan with water, sugar, and lemon zest and bring to a boil over high heat. Reduce to a simmer, cover partially, and cook until tender, 20 to 30 minutes.

2. Drain the tender pears, reserving the poaching liquid, and cool both completely.

3. Place the cooked pears in the bowl of a bar blender or food processor and process, slowly adding the poaching syrup. Continue processing, adding only as much syrup as is necessary to achieve a smooth puree. Pass the mixture through a fine-mesh strainer to remove unwanted fibers. Season with lemon juice and salt, then transfer the mixture to a freezable container.

4. Cover loosely with plastic or waxed paper and place in the freezer. Stir the mixture every 30 minutes until it starts to hold its shape. In about 4 hours it will have a scoopable consistency.

5. Scoop into chilled glasses or bowls and serve with fresh berries, caramel sauce, crushed pecan pralines, a whole poached pear (see next page) or a splash of Poire Williams. (Poire Williams is a classic French pear brandy. There are many brands and makers from around the world, but the French place clear glass bottles over the pear blossom, and let the fruit grow and ripen in the bottle. It's tremendously flavorful, and worth the extra bucks for special occasions— like homemade sorbet!)

Poached Pear Sorbet with
poached Bosc and Seckle pears

PEARS

Autumn is the season of the pear. There are dozens of varieties available, and all will make great sorbet. Classic poached pears are usually made with the Bosc pear, because it is firm and will hold its shape when cooked. It's a great pear for that purpose, but its flavor is unremarkable, and really needs a flavorful poaching liquid. Happily, because sorbet making means pureeing, the poached pear doesn't need to maintain its shape, which means you can choose any pear you like. Some of my favorites include the Anjou (short for Beurre d'Anjou), Comice (short for Doyenne du Comice), the Seckle, which is tiny but packed with a peppery punch, and the good ol' Bartlett, which is the American name for the Williams pear, incredibly flavorful when ripe. Go to a local market and have a taste test.

bananas foster sorbet

MAKES ABOUT 1 QUART OF SORBET

Bananas Foster is a classic sautéed banana dish made famous in the 1950s at Brennan's restaurant in New Orleans. Its signature element is a rum flambé, something you rarely see these days, as waiters cooking table-side has gone out of style. The classic flavors, however, are always in fashion.

INGREDIENTS

2 tablespoons (1 ounce) unsalted butter

¼ cup packed brown sugar

4 ripe bananas, peeled and sliced into ½-inch coins

Finely grated zest of 1 small lime

¼ cup rum (preferably Myers's)

Water, as needed

Juice of 1 small lime

Pinch of salt

METHOD

1. Melt the butter in large sauté pan over high heat. Add the brown sugar, and as it starts to melt, add the bananas. Reduce the heat to medium and stir the bananas around frequently as they begin to soften. Add the lime zest and continue to cook until the bananas have caramelized, 3 to 5 minutes. Add the rum, ignite (carefully), and allow the flame to burn out. Remove from the heat, and set aside to cool completely. (At this point, you could serve it as-is, as Bananas Foster.)

2. Place the cooled bananas and all the cooking liquid into a bar blender or food processor and process until smooth, adding cold water slowly as needed to facilitate the blending. Season with lime juice and salt, then transfer the mixture to a shallow freezable container.

3. Cover loosely with plastic or waxed paper and place in the freezer. Stir the mixture every 30 minutes until it starts to hold its shape. In about 4 hours it will have attained a scoopable consistency.

4. Scoop into chilled glasses or bowls and serve with caramel sauce, toasted coconut, warm grilled pineapple, rum cake, snickerdoodle cookies, or coconut macaroons.

VARIATIONS

SWIRL IT: Sorbet is not often swirled, but there is no good reason for that. It makes a great textural statement, especially when the swirl is an ooey-gooey caramel or fudge sauce. Drizzle

Bananas Foster Sorbet with
Bananas Foster

your sauce of choice between layers of already scoopable sorbet, and freeze for another hour before serving.

APPLES FOSTER: There is no such dessert as Apples Foster, but that doesn't mean you can't create one. Cook apples (or even pears) in the same manner as described above for bananas. Try replacing the rum with calvados or cognac. This makes a great topping, a base for fruit compote, or, as is the point here, a great sorbet. Use apple cider instead of water, as needed, to assist blending.

CINNAMON-BANANA: Add a few crushed cinnamon sticks, or ½ teaspoon of ground cinnamon to the bananas as they cook. Then, pass the base through a fine-mesh strainer before freezing to remove the sticks.

beet-pistachio sorbet

MAKES ABOUT 1 QUART OF SORBET

Beets are a root vegetable, of course, but they are also an important source of sugar. So you shouldn't be surprised to see it in a sorbet. Though it is slightly sweet, you can easily take it in either a sweet or savory direction. See page 154 for more Variations.

INGREDIENTS

1 cup sugar

1 cup water

1 cup shelled pistachios, finely chopped

4 large unpeeled beets, washed and quartered

Finely grated zest of 1 orange

Juice of ½ lemon

Pinch of salt

METHOD

1. Combine the sugar and water in a small saucepan and bring to a boil over high heat. When the syrup boils, remove it from the heat.

2. Meanwhile, preheat the oven to 350°F. Spread out the pistachios on a rimmed baking sheet and roast until golden and fragrant, about 10 minutes. Transfer the hot nuts directly to the warm syrup, and cool completely.

3. Place the beets in a large saucepan, cover with water, and bring to a boil over high heat. Cook until the beets are tender all the way through (a knife inserted should come out easily). Add extra water, as needed, to keep beets mostly submerged until they are cooked through. Drain the beets and set aside to cool.

4. Place the cooled beets and orange zest in the bowl of a blender or food processor and process until very smooth, adding the cooled pistachio simple syrup slowly, as needed, to facilitate the blending. Season with lemon juice and salt, then transfer the mixture to a shallow freezable container.

5. Cover loosely with plastic or waxed paper and place in the freezer. Stir the mixture every 30 minutes until it starts to hold its shape. In about 4 hours it will have a scoopable consistency.

6. Scoop into chilled glasses or bowls and serve with a drizzle of pistachio oil, rose-scented whipped cream, extra-dark chocolate sauce, candied orange zest, fried beet chips, candied rose petals, or pistachio tuile cookies.

APPETIZER BEET SORBET: Serve this delectable sorbet with a wedge of goat cheese and a salad of lightly dressed baby greens.

GOLDEN BEETS: Their flavor is similar, but their color is more fleeting. To prevent losing all the pigment in the boiling water, roast these beets whole instead. Wrap them together in a big sheet of aluminum foil and roast at 450°F until tender, about 1 hour. Then proceed with the recipe as directed.

Golden Beets Sorbet
with red beet chips and
chopped pistachios

carrot and ginger sorbet

The carrot is another ultrasweet vegetable that already has outstanding dessert references (in the form of cake). If you are lucky enough to find red, yellow, or purple carrots, by all means, use them here. And there is no better use for the carrots growing in your backyard. See pages 154–55 for Variations.

INGREDIENTS

1 cup sugar

1 cup water

Finely grated zest and juice of 1 orange

1 tablespoon of freshly grated peeled fresh ginger

4 cups roughly chopped unpeeled carrots

Juice of ½ lemon

Pinch of salt

METHOD

1. Combine the sugar, water, orange zest, orange juice, and ginger in a small saucepan and bring to a boil over high heat. When the syrup boils, remove it from the heat.

2. Meanwhile, place carrots in a large saucepan, cover with water, and bring to a boil over high heat. Cook until the carrots are tender all the way through (a knife inserted should come out easily). Add extra water, as needed, to keep carrots mostly submerged until they are cooked through. Drain the carrots and set aside to cool.

3. Place the cooled carrots in the bowl of a blender or food processor and process until very smooth, adding the gingered simple syrup slowly, as needed, to facilitate the blending. Pass the puree through a strainer to remove excess fiber, season with lemon juice and salt, then transfer the mixture to a shallow freezable container.

4. Cover loosely with plastic or waxed paper and place in the freezer. Stir the mixture every 30 minutes until it starts to hold its shape. In about 4 hours it will have attained a scoopable consistency.

5. Scoop into chilled glasses or bowls and serve with crème fraîche, caramel sauce, candied carrot ribbons, candied ginger, walnut lace cookies, dried fruit compote, coconut macaroons, or serve as an appetizer with a light carrot salad.

Carrot and Ginger Sorbet
with rainbow carrot salad

melon sorbet

MAKES ABOUT 1 QUART OF SORBET

There is only one good dessert that can be made from melons, and this is it. They are so full of water that any attempt to cook melons will result in disaster. Happily, melon sorbets come out great, and there are dozens of melon varieties you could conceivably use. Try this recipe with the holy trinity of brunch buffets: cantaloupe, honeydew, and watermelon. Then graduate to the more exotic varieties, available in the summer—Canary, Crenshaw, Casaba, Santa Claus, Sharlyn, Persian—and there are certainly specialty varieties in your area. Try them all! See page 155 for Variations.

INGREDIENTS

1 cup sugar

1 cup water

4 cups of melon chunks, skinned and seeded

Finely grated zest and juice of 1 small lemon or lime

Pinch of salt

METHOD

1. Combine the sugar and water in a small saucepan and bring to a boil over high heat. Remove from the heat and let cool completely.

2. Place the melon in the bowl of a bar blender or food processor and process until smooth, adding simple syrup slowly, as needed, to flavor and facilitate the blending. Be careful not to add an excessive amount of syrup. Melons are already sweet, and they have so much water that you won't need much to get it blended. Add the citrus zest, season with the juice and salt, then transfer the mixture to a shallow freezable container.

3. Cover loosely with plastic or waxed paper and place in the freezer. Stir the mixture every 30 minutes until it starts to hold its shape. In about 4 hours it will have attained a scoopable consistency.

4. Scoop into chilled glasses or bowls and serve with mixed melon ball salad (try adding peppercorns and tarragon or mint), fresh berries and yogurt, peppercorn-caramel glaze, chopped prosciutto, almond meringues, or a shot of vodka.

Melon Sorbet with
pepper-spiced melon balls

MELON

Melons are native to Africa and Asia, moving into Europe at the end of the Roman Empire. They are in the same botanical family as squash, gourds, and cucumbers (which makes sense when you think about their skin and seeds). Most of the melons we consider fruits are of the muskmelon variety, while many of the other varieties, including the bitter and kiwano melon, are commonly used in more savory applications, as with the cucumber. In Japan growers began controlling the shape of their melons. Square melons, grown inside clear cubes, are all the rage, and were supposedly created to stack easily and fit better in Japanese refrigerators. But since they are also growing heart-shaped and pyramid-shaped melons, each of which is selling for hundreds of dollars, I'm thinking there was another motivation.

sherbets

~~~~~~~

A sherbet (not sher-beRt) is essentially the same dessert as a sorbet, with one additional ingredient—dairy. Usually that ingredient is milk, but as you will see in this chapter, it can be done with a variety of milklike ingredients. The result is slightly less icy than a sorbet, but fresher than an ice cream. The addition of dairy also creates pastel colors that are a little bit daintier than the sorbet's bright hues.

cappuccino sherbet

If you like your coffee with cream, you will love this sherbet. It is milky and sweet, with just the right level of bitterness. Serve it in a big cappuccino mug with a dollop of whipped cream or meringue foam, a sprinkle of cinnamon, and a biscotti.

INGREDIENTS

1 cup sugar

3 cups milk

1 cup Italian dark roast coffee, ground coarse for drip machines

½ teaspoon fresh lemon juice

Pinch of salt

METHOD

1. Combine the sugar, milk, and ground coffee in a small saucepan and bring to a simmer over high heat. When at the simmer, remove from the heat, and set aside to cool completely. When cool, strain out grounds through a coffee filter or fine-mesh strainer lined with cheesecloth. Season with lemon juice and salt, and transfer to a shallow freezable container.

2. Cover loosely with plastic or waxed paper and place in the freezer. Stir the mix every 30 minutes until it starts to hold its shape. In about 4 hours it will have attained a scoopable consistency.

3. Scoop into chilled glasses or mugs and top with foamed milk, whipped cream, Italian meringue, caramel sauce, chocolate sauce, crushed almond toffee, candied orange, hazelnut brittle, biscotti, or snickerdoodles.

VARIATIONS

TURKISH COFFEE: Add some spice to the coffee bean milk for an exotic variation. Try it with 5 crushed cardamom pods, 2 pieces of star anise, and a cinnamon stick.

MOCHA: Pour the boiled coffee milk over 4 ounces of chopped chocolate and let it sit until melted. Stir until smooth, then proceed with the recipe as directed.

ITALIAN SYRUP: Add your favorite flavor of Italian syrup to the base just before it goes into the freezer.

fat-free chocolate sherbet

MAKES ABOUT 1 QUART OF SHERBET

I use to sell the hell out of this sherbet when I was a pastry chef. It tastes like a Fudgsicle, which is reason enough to try it, regardless of your current diet plan. You can also try this recipe with a sugar substitute, if you are determined to avoid all fun. See page 155 for more Variations.

INGREDIENTS

1 cup sugar

3 cups fat-free milk

½ cup unsweetened cocoa powder

Pinch of salt

METHOD

1. Combine the sugar and milk in a small saucepan and bring to a boil over high heat.

2. Put the cocoa powder in a small bowl and slowly drizzle in the hot milk while whisking, to create a smooth paste. Don't add it too fast or the mixture will get lumpy. Add the salt, then pass through a fine-mesh strainer to remove any lumps. Transfer the mixture to a shallow freezable container.

3. Cover loosely with plastic or waxed paper and place in the freezer. Stir the mix every 30 minutes until it starts to hold its shape. In about 4 hours it will have attained a scoopable consistency.

4. Scoop into chilled glasses or bowls, and top with orange suprêmes, raspberries, bananas, nonfat vanilla yogurt, angel food cake, or crisp hazelnut meringues.

VARIATIONS

SPICED CHOCOLATE: Steep the spices of your choice in the sweet warm milk. Try it with black pepper, cinnamon, chile flakes, cardamom, anise, or ginger. You can also give some herbs a try, including rosemary or tarragon.

COCONUT-CHOCOLATE: Canned unsweetened coconut milk has plenty of fat, but the addition here makes for some refreshing eating. Use it to replace the milk in the above recipe.

blood orange sherbet

MAKES ABOUT 1 QUART OF SHERBET

I love the blood orange. It's just so weird, how can you resist it? They say it is the result of a bee cross-pollinating an orange and a rose—whatever that means. I once worked for a chef who stained regular oranges with raspberries because the blood oranges were too expensive. Don't try that here. People will know. If you can't find the blood orange, just use an orange orange. See pages 155–56 for more Variations.

INGREDIENTS

½ cup sugar

2 cups fresh blood orange juice

Finely grated zest of 2 blood oranges

2 cups milk

Pinch of salt

METHOD

1. Combine the sugar, orange juice and zest in a small saucepan and bring to a boil over high heat. When the sugar has dissolved, remove from the heat and cool completely.

2. Once the orange juice is completely cool, stir in the milk and salt. It is important that it cool, otherwise the heat will cause the acidic juice to curdle. Transfer the mixture to a shallow freezable container.

3. Cover loosely with plastic or waxed paper and place in the freezer. Stir the mix every 30 minutes until it starts to hold its shape. In about 4 hours it will have attained a scoopable consistency.

4. Scoop into chilled glasses or bowls, and top with fresh suprêmes of blood oranges, pomegranate seeds, tropical fruit salsa, chocolate sauce, orange-caramel sauce, vanilla ice cream, black pepper tuile, almond toffee, sesame candy, or caramelize a plate of blood orange suprêmes with turbinado sugar and a blowtorch, then set a scoop on top.

VARIATION

BLOOD ORANGE FLOWER: Dainty this recipe up and add a teaspoon of orange flower water just before freezing.

agave-lime sherbet

MAKES ABOUT 1 QUART OF SORBET

*Agave is a syrup sweetener that has become all the rage because it supposedly has a lower gly-
cemic index than sugar, and it is all-natural, unlike non-nutritive sweeteners (see page 4). But
I like it because it has the subtle essence of tequila. Pair it with lime and you are very nearly
wasting away again in Margaritaville. You could add a jigger of tequila, but because alcohol
inhibits the freeze, agave is a better ingredient in a sorbet. Save the Hornitos for May 5. See page
156 for another Variation.*

INGREDIENTS

½ cup agave syrup

3 cups milk

Finely grated zest and juice
of 3 limes

Finely grated zest of ½
orange

¼ teaspoon orange flower
water

Pinch of kosher salt

METHOD

1. Add the agave and milk to a bowl and whisk vigorously to combine. Stir in lime, orange zest, orange flower water, and salt, then transfer to a shallow freezable container.

2. Cover loosely with plastic or waxed paper and place in the freezer. Stir the mix every 30 minutes until it starts to hold its shape. In about 4 hours it will have attained a scoopable consistency.

3. Scoop into chilled glasses with a sugared rim (dip first in lime juice), or serve it with a small shot of tequila and a few grinds of designer salt. You can also play down the tequila aspect, and play up the agave lime notes, by pairing this with a tropical fruit salsa, coconut whipped cream, or go in a savory direction and serve it over your best ceviche.

VARIATIONS

COCONUT-AGAVE: Replace the milk with an equal amount of canned unsweetened coconut milk.

CILANTRO-AGAVE: Omit the orange flower water and orange zest, then add ¼ cup finely chopped fresh cilantro leaves. (No stems please!) Serve this over fresh, lightly salted cucumbers for a hot summer day pick-me-up.

Coconut-Agave-Lime Sherbet

lavender-almond sherbet

Lavender is in the same family of herbs as rosemary, and you may detect a hint of it, especially when it is part of a savory mix, like herbes de Provence. But the floral tones lend themselves really well to sweet applications. In this recipe you can substitute cow's milk for almond milk if you are averse to nuts, or if you have trouble milking your almonds. See page 156 for Variations.

INGREDIENTS

1 cup sugar

3 cups almond milk

1 cup lavender buds

¼ vanilla bean, scraped

Finely grated zest of 1 lemon

Juice of 1 lemon

Pinch of salt

METHOD

1. Combine the sugar, almond milk, lavender, vanilla bean, and lemon zest in a small saucepan and bring to a boil over high heat. When the sugar has dissolved, remove from the heat and cool completely.

2. Strain the lavender buds out of the cooled milk, then season with lemon juice and salt. Transfer to a shallow freezable container.

3. Cover loosely with plastic or waxed paper and place in the freezer. Stir the mix every 30 minutes until it starts to hold its shape. In about 4 hours it will have attained a scoopable consistency.

4. Scoop into chilled glasses or bowls, and serve with whipped cream, almond brittle, poached pears, citrus-mint salsa, lemon ice box cookies, or compose it with another floral-infused frozen dessert of contrasting textures, such as Rosebud Ice Cream (page 36) or the Violet variation of infused Granita (page 123).

passion fruit, ginger, and carrot sherbet

MAKES ABOUT 1 QUART OF SHERBET

Passion fruit is one of the most overused items in the pastry kitchen. I think it's the name, but those who are especially new to the dessert arts tend to use the passion fruit with a heavy hand. This delicately floral, but highly acidic and tart fruit should be used with care so it doesn't overpower the rest of the plate. The passion fruit has big seeds, which are edible, but should be added to a dessert in moderation. Too many seeds look weird and wrong. See page 156 for Variations.

INGREDIENTS

2 cups carrot juice

½ cup sugar

One 1-inch piece fresh peeled ginger, chopped roughly

Finely grated zest of 1 lime

4 passion fruits, halved and scooped

1 cup whole milk

Juice of 1 lime

Pinch of salt

METHOD

1. Combine the carrot juice, sugar, ginger, and lime zest in a small saucepan and bring to a boil over high heat. When at the boil, remove from the heat. Scoop out the passion fruit pulp and add it to the warm carrot juice, then set aside to cool completely.

2. Pass the carrot-passion juice through a fine-mesh strainer to remove the ginger and the seeds. Add the milk to the strained juice, season with lime juice and salt, then transfer to a shallow freezable container.

3. Cover loosely with plastic or waxed paper and place in the freezer. Stir the mix every 30 minutes until it starts to hold its shape. In about 4 hours it will have attained a scoopable consistency.

4. Scoop into chilled glasses or bowls, and serve with mango slices, candied carrot ribbons, coconut whipped cream, coconut macaroons, or scoop into coconut lace cookie taco shells.

persimmon sherbet

Another seasonal fruit, the persimmon is a call to fall. In the autumn persimmons are treated much like pumpkins or sweet potatoes, paired with winter spices, and turned into pies, cakes, and muffins. But a fresh ripe persimmon is a delicious thing on its own, and deserves a little spotlight. If persimmons are new to you, be sure to read the note about choosing the right fruit. See page 156 for Variations.

INGREDIENTS

2 cups whole milk

¼ cup sugar

1 Darjeeling tea bag (or another black tea)

3 cups chopped ripe persimmon (about 6 fruits)

Finely grated zest of 1 lemon

Juice of 1 lemon

Pinch of salt

METHOD

1. Combine the milk, sugar, tea bag, and persimmons in a small saucepan and bring to a boil over high heat. When at the boil, remove from the heat and drain off the liquid and reserve, then let each component cool completely. Let the tea bag steep in the milk until cool.

2. Place the persimmons and lemon zest in a bar blender or food processor and process to a smooth puree. Add the sweet tea–milk mixture slowly to facilitate the puree. Pass the mixture through a fine-mesh strainer to remove the excess fibers. Season with lemon juice and salt, then transfer to a shallow freezable container.

3. Cover loosely with plastic or waxed paper and place in the freezer. Stir the mix every 30 minutes until it starts to hold its shape. In about 4 hours it will have attained a scoopable consistency.

4. Scoop into chilled glasses or bowls and serve with candied lemon peel, pomegranate seeds, fresh berries, ruby red grapefruit suprêmes, fortune cookie tuile, almond shortbread, or sandwich it between two slices of pound cake, with an additional spoonful of raspberry jam inside.

Persimmon Sherbet sandwiched with pound cake and raspberry jam

PERSIMMONS

Also known as lantern fruit, the persimmon ripens in the fall, after the leaves from their trees drop, leaving the fruit behind hanging like delicate orange Chinese lanterns. There are two varieties of persimmons readily available to us in the fall. The Hachiya persimmon is an acorn-shaped fruit that ripens soft with dark splotches on the skin, which is an indication of sugar inside. This is the astringent variety, meaning that until it is soft and ripe it is not edible. If you try to eat it before it ripens its astringency coats your whole mouth, tongue, and throat, which is not at all pleasant. The squat, tomato-shaped Fuyu, on the other hand, is sweet while still firm. This aspect makes it a nice choice for eating raw, as in a salad, salsa, or compote. For this dessert I prefer the perfectly ripe Hachiya variety, for no other reason than they are easier to puree. You can use either in this recipe.

thai iced tea sherbet

MAKES ABOUT 1 QUART OF SHERBET

Thai iced tea definitely negates any healthy advantage one might receive from eating Thai food. It is really just tea with sweetened condensed milk. Of course, their tea is really, really good. See page 157 for Variations.

INGREDIENTS

1 cup sugar

2 cups milk

½ cup loose-leaf black tea

4 pieces star anise

4 cardamom pods, crushed

1 tablespoon crushed dried tamarind or tamarind paste

2 tablespoons sweetened condensed milk

1 teaspoon fresh lemon juice

Pinch of salt

METHOD

1. Combine the sugar, milk, tea, anise, and cardamom in a small saucepan and bring to a simmer over high heat. When at the simmer, remove from the heat and let cool completely. When cool, strain out and discard the tea leaves and spices.

2. Stir in the tamarind and sweetened condensed milk. Season with lemon juice and salt, then place in a shallow freezable container.

3. Cover loosely with plastic or waxed paper and place in the freezer. Stir the mix every 30 minutes until it starts to hold its shape. In about 4 hours it will have attained a scoopable consistency.

4. Scoop into chilled glasses or bowls, and top with fresh mint, whipped cream, coconut cream, candied ginger, mango slices, boba, or use in a duo with coconut granita.

TAMARIND

Known as the Indian date, the edible pods from the tamarind tree contain a pulp that is tart when green, and sweeter, but still a bit sour, when ripe. It is used widely throughout the world in jams, beverages, desserts, salty snacks, and sauces, including Worcestershire. The pods (technically a tree legume) are often available fresh in ethnic markets, but more readily available, and easier to use, as a dried paste. Heat the paste in a little water to soften, then remove the pits and fibers. You can use tamarind as you would a tart fruit like cranberries, or use it as you would lemon juice or vinegar, to brighten natural flavors with an exotic tang.

Thai Iced Tea Sherbet with boba

indian rose water sherbet

MAKES ABOUT 1 QUART OF SHERBET

I always have a bottle of rose water on hand. It is a wonderful addition to all kinds of foods. Rose simple syrup is lovely in tea, lemonade, and cocktails; it's nice added to fruit jams or to rice for your favorite curry dishes. But most of all, it makes great desserts. See page 157 for an additional Variation.

INGREDIENTS

2 to 3 saffron threads

3 cups milk or almond milk

1 cup sugar

2 crushed cardamom pods

Finely grated zest of ½ lemon

2 tablespoons rose water

Juice of ½ lemon

Pinch of salt

METHOD

1. Toast the saffron threads on a hot dry skillet for 20 to 30 seconds until crispy. Remove from the heat immediately and cool.

2. Combine the milk, sugar, cardamom, lemon zest, and saffron in a small saucepan and bring to a boil over high heat. When the sugar has dissolved, remove from the heat and cool completely.

3. Strain the spices out of the cooled milk, then add the rose water and season with lemon juice and salt. Transfer to a shallow freezable container.

4. Cover loosely with plastic or waxed paper and place in the freezer. Stir the mix every 30 minutes until it starts to hold its shape. In about 4 hours it will have attained a scoopable consistency.

5. Scoop into chilled glasses or bowls, and top with fresh berries, mango slices, sautéed stone fruits, dried raisin compote, almond shortbread, or use it to top coconut rice pudding, lemon pound cake, or blackberry pie.

VARIATIONS

CARROT-ROSE: Replace a cup of milk with a cup of carrot juice for a delicious and beautiful orange-colored variation.

ROSE PETAL: Omit the saffron and replace it with extra rose in the form of dried rosebuds, available in most Mexican, Middle Eastern, and Indian markets. Crush the buds, sift out any stems, and add about 2 tablespoons to the sherbet as it freezes.

other easy
frozen desserts

～～～～

There is more to be done with ice cream than just plopping it into a cone! Here are more fun ideas to consider adding to your repertoire.

GRANITA

Granita is considered an Italian dessert, although, like most things, it has similar incarnations around the world. It is frequently lumped into a category of snow cones or shaved ice, in which flavored syrups or fruit juices are added after ice crystals are gathered, like Nero did (see Introduction). But in granita the water itself is flavored before it becomes ice.

The Japanese have a similar dessert, *kakigōri*, which they brought with them to Hawaii. Cuba's variation, *granizados*, which is found throughout Miami, comes from the Spanish word for "hailstones." Dominicans call their snow cones *frío frío*. Hawaiian shaved ice is closely related to desserts in East Asia that are flavored with sweet condensed milk, sweet red adzuki beans, or custard. (I could wax poetic for days about Hawaiian shaved ice.) Mexico, Colombia, and Venezuela have *raspa*, which is the word for "scrape." Puerto Rican *piragua* is named for the pyramid shape they are scooped into. In the Philippines they have *halo-halo* ("mix mix"), while Thailand has *Nam Kang Sai*. Many cultures top their icy desserts with sweetened condensed milk or custard sauce (sometimes just called cream or crème), sweet beans, glutinous rice, and fresh or pureed fruits.

Sicily claims a specific variety of this dessert, which is slightly different, and a little chunkier than the granita found across the rest of Italy. The difference lies in the preparation: a thin liquid is stirred periodically as it freezes, which creates large ice crystals. In other parts of Italy you will find granita that is more akin to sorbet, passed through an ice cream (or gelato) machine.

Sicilian granita is set apart from the others, too, by its flavors, including coffee, almond, bitter almond, mandarin, lemon, jasmine, mint, mulberries, and a chocolate version that is found in Catania, but pretty much nowhere else.

Although many chefs consider granita to be "the lazy-cook's dessert," there is a definite place for these delicate ice crystals on your menu. They are quick, to be sure. They are, in fact, the original "No-Churn." But there is some skill involved. The cool crystals are as ephemeral as a food can get. If you don't plan it right,

Midway through forking Pomegranate Granita

your granita will melt before it even hits the table. The key is in the planning.

The short life of granita can be put to advantage. Flavored with herbs and olive oil as a frozen dressing, it can be served with much fanfare atop a plate of baby greens, or a dish of ceviche on a hot summer day. Or serve it alongside something hot, and experience it deliciously melting on your tongue. I am particularly fond of granita as an accompaniment to other desserts of contrasting textures. Topped with whipped cream, it is a delight on the tongue. In Sicily, espresso granita topped with almond cream is a standard breakfast item.

Pair granita with a creamy ice cream in a complementary, or contrasting, flavor. Pair it with extra-rich desserts as a welcome respite from cloying, sweetened fat. Scoop it atop fresh ripe fruits, or use it as a palate cleanser, as you would a traditional sorbet.

The method is identical in each recipe. Create a flavored water, put it in the freezer in a shallow pan, and

mix up the ice crystals with a fork (affectionately referred to as "forking") every 20 minutes until the entire
pan is frozen into a loose mass of ice crystals (about
90 minutes, depending on your freezer). It should be
more on the dry side than slushy, and once it is ready,
it should be served. If it freezes for an extended period
unforked, the crystals will fuse, and you will be left with
a delicious block of ice. (If it becomes a block of ice, you
have the choice of melting and reforking, or scraping it
into a snowy shave-ice texture—not a bad dessert, but
not granita.)

If you plan on serving the granita as the main event,
be sure that your glasses, bowls, or dishes are frozen, too.
Put them in the freezer 30 to 60 minutes before serving.
When the granita hits the frozen dish, it will live longer
outside of the freezer.

The following are a few ideas for granita. There are
slight variations in the preparation of the liquid itself,
but the freezing techniques are identical.

Sicilian Granita Vinaigrette over mixed greens

classic sicilian granita

MAKES ABOUT 1 QUART OF GRANITA

*Use whatever liquid you like. Fruit juices make an easy first try,
because they require no adjustment. Once you see how easy it
is, you'll want to start creating your own flavors by using teas,
herbs, spices, fruit juices, vegetable juices, and cocktails. See
below for these Variations, and page 157 for another.*

INGREDIENTS

4 cups liquid
½ to 1 cup simple syrup, or as needed if using
coffee, tea, or other unsweetened liquid
1 teaspoon fresh lemon juice
Pinch of salt to season

METHOD

1. Mix all the ingredients and place in a shallow baking
dish and set it in the freezer. Use a fork to mix up the ice
crystals every 20 minutes until the entire pan is frozen
and slushy, about 90 minutes.

2. Serve as-is, or as a part of a composed dish. Be sure to
use chilled glasses so it doesn't melt too soon.

VARIATIONS

BOOZY GRANITA: Vin Santo is a sweet Italian
dessert wine that is commonly made into granita. The
low alcohol content makes the freezing possible. If you'd
like to create a champagne-, wine-, beer-, or cocktail-
inspired granite, do so with the alcohol content in
mind. If the freeze seems to be slow in coming, add some
plain cold water or other liquid to dilute the alcohol.

INFUSIONS: Teas, coffees, flowers, herbs, and
spices can all be prepared in this manner.

Combine the infusible you want with the water,
and with sugar, lemon juice, and salt. Bring to a boil
briefly, remove from the heat, and set aside to steep and
cool completely. Strain into a shallow baking dish and
proceed with the recipe as directed. Consider steeping
lavender, violets, roses, chamomile, black or green teas,
kaffir lime leaves, lemongrass, citrus zest, and any other
herb or spice you can imagine.

nut granita

Nut granitas have a long tradition in Italy. Almond (mandorla) or bitter almond (which can be replicated using apricot pits!) is standard, as are hazelnut and walnut. I toast the nuts first, without exception. Heat brings the nut's natural oils to the surface, and adds a rich toastiness. Adding the nuts to the milk while they are still hot helps infuse their flavor into the milk, and allowing them to sit as long as possible ensures maximum flavor transfer. Chopping the nuts prior to toasting opens up maximum surface area, and more opportunities for flavor to escape into the milk.

INGREDIENTS

2 cups toasted chopped nuts (still warm)
4 cups nonfat milk
½ cup sugar, or more as needed
1 teaspoon fresh lemon juice
Pinch of salt to season

METHOD

1. Preheat the oven to 350°F. Spread chopped nuts out on a rimmed baking sheet in a single layer and bake until they smell toasty, and have turned golden brown. This may require a bit of stirring, but should only take about 10 minutes. Keep warm.

2. Meanwhile, bring the milk and sugar to a boil in a large saucepan. When at the boil, remove from the heat immediately, and add the hot nuts right away. Stir, then set aside to steep and cool completely. (If you can do this step a day ahead, the flavor will be that much more intense.)

3. When completely cool, strain the nuts out of the milk, squeezing out all the moisture you can. Place the nut milk in a shallow baking dish, add the lemon juice and salt, and set it in the freezer. Use a fork to mix up the ice crystals every 20 minutes until the entire pan is frozen and slushy, about 90 minutes.

4. Serve as-is, or as a part of a composed dessert. Be sure to use chilled glasses so it doesn't melt too soon (see page 123).

fruit puree granita

Fruits can be tricky to put in granita form. Their pulps are frequently too thick, producing a sorbet—which, while good, is a different thing. (See page 89.) Choose fruit with a thinner pulp for the best results.

INGREDIENTS

2 cups fruit
2 cups water
½ cup sugar, or more as needed
1 teaspoon fresh lemon juice
Pinch of salt to season

METHOD

1. Puree the fruits in a blender with water, sugar, lemon juice, and salt until smooth. Pass through a fine-mesh strainer into a shallow baking dish. Adjust the seasoning, and add more water, as needed, to create a thin juice. Place the pan in the freezer.

2. Use a fork to mix up the ice crystals every 20 minutes until the entire pan is frozen and slushy, about 2 hours.

3. Serve as-is, or as a part of a composed dessert. Be sure to use chilled glasses so it doesn't melt too soon.

VARIATIONS

Some fruits work better than others. Melons are great for this application, as are citrus fruits, pomegranates,

---

ACID

Acid is like salt, it can bring out fresh flavor, but don't use it with such a heavy hand that you can tell it's there. For neutral flavor enhancement, I use lemon, champagne, or white wine vinegar. For darker flavors, like berries or red wine, use a balsamic or red wine vinegar. For tropical flavors I usually use lime juice, but rice vinegar works too. For autumnal flavors, like pumpkin or apple, use apple cider vinegar.

---

kiwis, and a variety of berries. Those with thicker pulps, such as mangos and stone fruits, are best left for sorbet, unless you thin them way down. The problem with thinning, though, is that you also thin the flavor. "The more you know."

COMPOSED DESSERTS

"Composition" is a "cheffy" way to say "built." This section shows you how to build some classic ice cream–based desserts.

baked alaska

MAKES 4 BAKED ALASKAS

This is perhaps the most fun dessert ever created. The Baked Alaska we know today is a variation of a classic dish known for centuries to the Chinese, Norwegians, and French, who undoubtedly were the ones who turned Thomas Jefferson on to it. The version here was put on the menu at Delmonico's Restaurant in New York City in 1876 to celebrate Alaska, the newest American territory. The ice cream is set on a foundation of cake, completely encapsulated in meringue, then baked to set and brown the meringue. The idea is that the meringue is an insulator, keeping the ice cream cold during baking.

INGREDIENTS

Four slices of cake, serving-sized, about 1 inch thick. (Try cutting pieces with a 2- to 3-inch round biscuit cutter, or into a similar size square.)
Four scoops of ice cream
4 large egg whites
A pinch of salt
8 ounces sugar

METHOD

1. Place one ice cream scoop on top of each slice of cake, and place them in the freezer to harden.
2. Place a small saucepan half full of water over high heat and bring to a boil. Combine the egg whites, salt, and sugar in the bowl of a stand mixer, or another heatproof bowl. When the water boils, reduce to a simmer, and place the bowl of egg whites on top. Stir slowly and continuously until the whites are slightly warmed and the sugar has dissolved, 1 to 2 minutes. Be careful not to let the egg whites cook!
3. Remove the bowl from the heat and whip the egg whites until stiff peaks form and the mixture is cool.
4. Transfer the meringue to a piping bag. Working with one ice cream scoop at a time, pipe the meringue in concentric rings, starting at the base, next to the cake, and winding up to the top of the ice cream scoop. Conceal all the ice cream, so all that can be seen is a snowy dome of meringue. Return the Alaska to the freezer while you prepare the remaining scoops. (You can use a plain or star tip in your pastry bag if you wish, or simply use a metal spreading spatula to create a more rustic pattern. You can also touch a rubber spatula to the meringue and pull it away quickly, creating spikes of white.) The dessert can be held in the freezer for several hours in this state.
5. Brown the meringue in one of three ways. Bake briefly in a very hot oven (450°F) until browned (about 5 minutes), brown with a propane or butane torch, or

Baked Alaska

top the meringue with a teaspoon of liqueur and ignite it with a match at the table. Take care with the last option that you don't light your guests on fire.

Chocolate Ice Cream sandwiched in peanut butter cookies, rolled in peanuts on the edges

ICE CREAM SANDWICHES, CONES, AND CAKES

ICE CREAM SANDWICHES

As of this writing, there is a huge ice cream sandwich trend. Shops are opening up all over, and restaurants are serving ice cream sandwiches composed of fabulous ice cream inside of doughnuts, croissants, macaroons—you name it.

I grew up eating the "It's-It," made in San Francisco. It was simply a really great oatmeal cookie with vanilla ice cream, dipped in chocolate. Over the years, they added flavors, but the original vanilla has always been the best. All over Sicily they do an amazing thing with a brioche bun—it looks more like a gelato burger than a sandwich, but it is crazy good. A similar thing is done in Southeast Asia, although their ice cream is more likely to be flavored with yam, red adzuki beans, or durian. In the British Isles the ice cream is more likely to be sandwiched between thin cookie wafers, and will often have an interior hidden bonus of nougat or caramel.

Lots of ice cream companies already make sandwiches, but they are superfun and oh-so-satisfying to make at home. You can sandwich your ice cream with anything. The following are some ideas to get your sandwich creativity flowing, and a few tips to make it easier and better.

Outer Layers

COOKIES: Of course, chocolate chip and oatmeal are great. But how about a coconut macaroon with mango ice cream? Or a gingersnap with pumpkin ice cream? Any cookie can work, so open your mind to the sandwich possibilities.

BARS: How about a brownie sandwich? Or a blondie? Or a lemon bar sandwich? (Be sure to face the lemon top of the bars inward for easy handling.)

PASTRY DOUGH: Got a little leftover pie dough? An extra cream puff? Spare puff pastry? I didn't think so, but if you did they would make great sandwich material too. Try baking puff pastry squares with a dusting of granulated sugar. Or a thin sugar tart dough (*pâte sucré*) cut in delicate circles. Or make cream puffs (*pâte à choux*), and fill them with ice cream. This is technically called a profiterole, but when you're the cook you get to call it whatever you want.

CAKE: Sliced cake makes a great sandwich. In my pastry chef days we made a loaf of pound cake, sliced it like bread, and filled it with chocolate ice cream and fresh raspberries, then cut on the diagonal like a PB&J. Any cake will work, but they are easier to form when baked in a loaf pan. (FYI, you can bake any cake in a loaf pan.) For added stability, toast the cake slices (and cool them) before sandwiching. Try lemon pound cake with rose ice cream, carrot cake with ginger ice cream, angel food cake with fat-free chocolate sherbet, or pumpkin spice cake with cranberry-pomegranate sorbet.

BREAD: As I mentioned, brioche is king of the ice cream sandwich in Sicily. It works well because it is a rich dough (a technical term that means it has a lot of fat in it). And any other rich dough works great as a sandwich—croissants, cinnamon rolls, raisin bread, bear claws, Christmas stollen, panettone, Easter kulich, challah—you really can't go wrong with any of these.

Lean bread, with no fat, will work, too, but it may need help from toasting and smearing. Try sourdough toast, Nutella, and chocolate ice cream. Or rosemary bread with apple butter and rum-raisin ice cream. Or whole wheat toast with marmalade and orange-mint ice cream. Yum.

BROWN DERBY

The Brown Derby is a chocolate-dipped ice cream cone (because the chocolate looks like a hat—get it?). While it traditionally refers to a soft-serve cone, the description still applies to traditional scoops.

SOME TIPS

If you are baking the outer portion (cookies or cakes or whatever) for your sandwich, do not do your sandwiching while they are hot. Or warm. Not even the least little bit warm. The ice cream will melt. When you think they are completely cool, chill them down even more in the freezer for 30 minutes before you sandwich.

Sandwich your ice cream at least an hour before you want to eat it. This allows the ice cream to firm up, which prevents the ice cream from oozing out of the sandwich as you bite it, therefore preserving your dignity, and probably your shirt. If you really can't wait that long, make a little baby one for yourself to taste right away.

Don't use too big a cookie or piece of cake. It should easily fit in your hand. Even if you intend to serve it as a plated dessert, hand-sized is a good serving size, and will make it easier to eat with a fork (or fingers).

Don't overfill! A standard ice cream scoop is the recommended amount of ice cream. As I stated above, it's a good serving size, and it makes eating easier.

There are several options for the material of your hat. I like to use thin ganache, made with extra cream, and cooled, but still liquid. You can also use straight melted chocolate, thinned down with cocoa butter, coconut oil, or vegetable oil, and then cooled. Chocolate sauces will not harden unless they are refrozen. And then there is the "shell" product available at the supermarket, which consists of magic fast-drying mystery food. (It's not that big of a mystery. My first job at the age of fifteen was at an ice cream parlor. Part of my job was adding paraffin to the "dip.")

To dip a cone, it is important that your ice cream not fall off into the chocolate. Press the scoops firmly into the cones. (That means don't buy cheap cones.) I like to scoop the cones, then freeze them again for a little while just for insurance. Dip the cone quickly, then re-dip it in chopped nuts, toasted coconut, sprinkles, jimmies, or cookie crumbs.

Strawberry Brown Derby

ICE CREAM CAKES

Ice cream cakes are nothing but giant ice cream sandwiches. Here's how to do it:

1. Make the ice cream of your choice.

2. Make the cake of your choice in a round or square pan. Bake either 2 thin cakes, or one thick one that you can cut in half horizontally. Cool the cake completely. (You can, of course, make more layers if you want to.)

3. To assemble, use the same size cake pan that you baked the cake in. Line it with a long sheet of plastic wrap that can be wrapped across the top after the cake is fully assembled.

4. Place one thin layer of cake into the pan. Brush on a soaking syrup if you are using one. Scoop ice cream on top of cake, in an even layer. Press down to pack out air. Top with second layer of cake. Press gently, and brush again with soaking syrup. Wrap in plastic wrap, then freeze for 1 to 2 hours.

5. Whip up a frosting. The type you choose will depend on the flavors of your cake and ice cream, but the easiest are plain sweetened whipped cream (crème Chantilly), page 133, or soft chocolate ganache (page 134). Of course, any frosting you love will work fine. Unwrap and unmold cake onto a serving plate. Cover evenly with frosting, then put it back into the freezer until serving time.

VARIATIONS

Some ideas to get your ice cream cake ideas flowing:

CREAMSICLE CAKE: Vanilla/white cake, vanilla soaking syrup, orange sherbet, whipped cream frosting.

ICED CAPPUCCINO CAKE: Chocolate cake, coffee soaking syrup, coffee ice cream, chocolate ganache or coffee-flavored whipped cream.

PIÑA COLADA CAKE: Coconut cake, pineapple ice cream, rum soaking syrup, coconut cream frosting, covered in shredded coconut.

Ice Cream Cake with Raspberry Sorbet, Blackberry Gelato, and Blueberry Ice Cream, frosted with whipped cream

FROZEN FRUIT BOWLS

I stole this idea from my mommy, who no doubt got
it straight out of a 1965 *Good Housekeeping* magazine.
Hollowed-out fruits make fun and clever containers for
your frozen desserts. The classic is an orange, but there
are a few other things you can do in a similar way.

ORANGE BOWL

1. Cut the bottom off an orange, on the stem end,
just enough to flatten the base so it doesn't roll.

2. Cut off and remove the top of the oranges (ap-
proximately $1/6$ inch).

3. Scoop out the center meat. Use a grapefruit
spoon if you have one. It has tiny teeth on the edges
designed for scraping out citrus.

4. Fill the hollowed-out fruit with a generous scoop
of ice cream, then refreeze for 15 to 30 minutes.

5. Serve directly from the freezer. As it arrives at
the table it will become frosty. Consider an accompany-
ing whipped cream or sauce.

VARIATIONS

ANY OTHER SERVING-SIZE FRUIT: Any citrus.
An apple or pear. A persimmon. Hollow out in the same
manner as above.

A PINEAPPLE: Really! Cut in half vertically and
hollow out. Fill each half with ice cream, packed in

well and smoothed on top, flush with the pineapple.
Refreeze for 2 to 3 hours, then cut wedges for serving.

A MELON: Use the same method as the pineapple
above. Leave an inch or so of melon fruit on the
rind, then use a contrasting-colored melon sorbet.
Crazy!

ICE BOWLS

This is a fun idea for serving ice cream at a party. A
bowl made out of ice! (I think I also stole this idea from
the 1960s.)

1. Take two stainless steel bowls of a graduated size.
Fill the large bowl with berries, flowers, leaves, herbs,
cinnamon sticks—whatever corresponds to your ice
cream flavor, or the season. Add enough ice (cubes or
crushed) to fill the bowl by half.

2. Place the smaller bowl on top of the ice. Press
it down so the ice and garnishes fill the space between the two bowls, forming a bowl shape. Use a
can of soup or something freezeable to weigh down
the little bowl, which will keep it from floating in
the next step.

3. Fill the large bowl with water. The garnish and
ice will shift a bit, so make any necessary adjustments,
then bring the whole thing to the freezer. Freeze it overnight until it is solid.

4. To serve, remove from the freezer, take out the
weight, and fill the little bowl with a little cold water.
It should pop right out. Turn the big bowl upside down,
and pour a little cold water over the back of the bowl,
and the ice will also pop right out. Refreeze until you
are ready to serve.

5. Place it on a lipped tray with a cloth napkin at
the base to keep it steady, and to catch the water as it
melts throughout the night.

toppings
and
accompaniments

Sure, ice cream is fine all by itself. But it always dances better with a partner. Why do you think the cone was invented? Not only so you could hold it in your hand (and eat the bowl!) but also because the crisp wafer was a perfect accompaniment to the creamy custard. And that is much of the secret to good food pairing—opposites. Opposite textures, temperatures, flavors, even opposite colors and sizes make for interesting eating. Besides, if you dress it up right, no one will ever know you took the shortcut!

BASICS OF MENU DEVELOPMENT

PLANNING YOUR PLATE

The first thing to do when creating a dish is to look around. What is being served at the rest of the meal? Is it themed in some way? If the food is from a particular culture or region, you'll want to try to stick to that theme at dessert. That doesn't mean you have to alter your original flavor idea, just adjust the interpretation by its accompaniments. For instance, you can serve chocolate ice cream and make it fit into an Italian context by serving it with espresso or amaretto flavors. For French, try incorporating Grand Marnier, or turn it into a classic profiterole. South-of-the-Border chocolate is infused with cinnamon, or paired with chiles.

Of course, it's nice when your main flavor ideas take their cues from a particular region. Finish an Indian meal with saffron ice cream, rose granita, fresh mangos, and coconut tuiles. A Thai dinner can end with coconut ice cream, lemongrass and kaffir lime– infused caramel sauce, and oven-dried pineapple "flowers." Finish off your barbecue with apple pie ice cream in an oatmeal cookie sandwich. You get the idea.

Is it a holiday or celebration? Make sure you are choosing flavors that the birthday boy or happy couple prefers. (Yes, people do order their favorite cakes for other people.) Calendar holidays are the most fun for pastry chefs, because there are already ascribed flavors. Not that you are obliged to stick to them. I could go my entire life without another "red, white, and blueberry" dessert on the Fourth of July.

And don't forget about the season. The best possible composition includes foods that are ripe right then. Sure, we can get just about anything anytime (strawberries and melon come to mind), but that doesn't mean that they are good, nor does it mean that such a thing is socially responsible. Take a trip to your farmers' market (or farm) and support your local growers. (It will help ensure you have good fresh produce for years to come.)

An important point to make here is that you do not have to always follow a recipe to a "T." Substitutions are encouraged, especially if they are seasonal. So if peaches are out of season, use pears instead. No raspberries? Try cranberries or pomegranates. It is necessity that breeds creativity. Someone said that—not me. (Although, yes, I did just say that.)

GARNISHING

There is a great deal of satisfaction derived from your guests' wide-eyed looks of delight when a plate brought to the table looks amazing. Delicious food will always be appreciated, but good-looking food is something to cherish. It means that the host really cares about the food, and about the guest.

Garnishing can be as simple as a fresh herb sprig or as complicated as a caramel sugar cage. The trick to making it right is to have it make sense. Although practically every two-bit restaurant sticks a sprig of mint on every dessert (for color—but I say who mandated that every plate needs green?), mint rarely makes sense with the flavor of most desserts. Garnishes should not only be edible, but should complement the flavor of the dessert. That means there is no need for spun sugar on a brownie. A few fresh berries, a dust of powdered sugar, or a dollop of cream could, however, be lovely. Choose flavors and textures that complement and contrast with crunch, cream, warmth, or chill.

FLUFFY TOPPINGS

One of the best accompaniments to frozen desserts is something fluffy and light. The technical know-how makes it special, the textural difference makes it delicious.

swiss meringue

MAKES ABOUT 4 CUPS MERINGUE

This technique heats the eggs enough to render them safe, and the heat acts as a stabilizer so there is less of a chance that you will overwhip.

french meringue

MAKES ABOUT 4 CUPS MERINGUE

This is the basic meringue. Use it for crisp baked meringues, or to fold into other recipes.

INGREDIENTS

2 egg whites

Pinch of salt

¼ cup sugar

METHOD

1. Place the egg whites and salt in a large mixing bowl and whip vigorously until soft peaks appear.

2. Slowly begin adding the sugar, a teaspoon at a time, while whipping, until all the sugar has been added and the meringue is at a stiff peak.

MERINGUES

Fluffy whipped egg whites are an ethereal treat and not hard to make. There are a couple rules to follow, though; these are found in the Introduction.

There are three types of meringue. French meringue is the simplest (it is sometimes referred to as "simple" or "common" meringue), and involves the slow addition of granulated sugar to whipping egg whites. This is the easiest, but it is not very stable, and it is easily overwhipped. More important, it is not cooked. That means that it is typically only used in recipes that will get cooked, such as sponge cakes, or crisp meringue cookies, wafers, or bowls, which are a good contrast with creamy ice cream.

Italian meringue makes a great topping, as-is, for super-tart desserts. Dolloped like whipped cream, the sweet creamy texture perfectly offsets icy sorbets. It is a bit more challenging to make, as it involves a hot sugar syrup. Swiss meringue can be used as-is, or baked until crisp, which is why it is my favorite.

TESTING PEAKS

The term "peak" refers to the appearance of mountains of meringue or cream that are created by the incorporation of air. The more air that goes into these ingredients, the stiffer they will become. To judge a peak, dip a spoon in, scoop out a little bit, then hold it upright, so that the meringue or cream points to the sky. If the very tip of the peak points straight up, it's a stiff peak. If it droops over a little, it's a medium peak. If it flops way over, or doesn't peak at all, it's soft peak.

italian meringue

The most stable, and the most beautiful meringue, is the Italian meringue. This is also known in parts of the United States as 7-Minute Icing, or White Mountain Icing. It is the same principle as the Swiss version, but rather than heating the eggs and sugar together, the sugar is cooked into a syrup, and added hot to the whipping whites.

It requires that you cook sugar to soft-ball stage. If you have a phobia of cooking sugar, or have never tried it before, this is the perfect opportunity for you to master the technique, because the recipe is small, and there is not much to lose if you screw it up. You might want to read about cooking sugar first on page 158.

INGREDIENTS

¼ cup sugar

2 tablespoons water

2 to 3 drops of fresh lemon juice

2 egg whites

Pinch of salt

METHOD

1. In a very small saucepan, combine the sugar and water. Mix together so that it resembles wet sand. Be sure to wipe all traces of sugar off the inside of the pan. (Use wet fingers for this so you can feel where the sugar granules are.) Set over high heat and bring to a boil. Do not move or stir the pan at all.

2. When at the boil, add the lemon juice. Do not stir—the bubbles will mix it in. Cook until the syrup reaches soft-ball stage. (Cook for 5 minutes at full boil, then check the stage; see the chart on pages 158–59 for help.)

3. As the sugar begins to cook, in a separate bowl whip the egg whites and salt until they reach medium-firm peak.

4. When the sugar syrup is at the soft-ball stage, immediately remove it from the heat and drizzle it into the whipping whites (already at medium peak). Drizzle in gradually in a slow, steady stream, taking about 30 seconds to complete. When pouring into a stand mixer, try to pour the stream of sugar between

> The most common mistake in making Italian meringue is taking the sugar too far. Sugar in hardball or crack stages will solidify on the inside of the bowl and on the whisk, resulting in whipped eggs with chunks of sugar. If this happens, chalk it up to experience and try again. Practice makes perfect.

the whipping whip and the side of the bowl. If it hits the whip, you will spin it like cotton candy, which is fun, but doesn't suit our purposes here. Hand whippers can be a little less precise, but you need to keep the action moving until all the sugar has been added.

5. Continue whipping on high speed until the whites are at stiff peak. The meringue is now ready to use.

sweetened whipped cream (crème chantilly)

Whipped cream is the all-purpose, go-to topping. In French it's called crème Chantilly (Shahn-tee-ee), and it is subtly flavored with sugar and vanilla. When you create this accompaniment, be sure to consider the dessert you are preparing. Really sweet desserts benefit from only slightly sweetened cream. Some are better with the touch of acidity provided by a tablespoon or two of sour cream or crème fraîche. And tart desserts—like those featuring lime or lemon, can tolerate more sugar. The following recipe is just a guideline. Use your own palate for real guidance. If you don't whip much, it might be useful to review the information about creams and whipping, pages 3 and 7 in the Introduction.

INGREDIENTS

2 cups heavy cream, cold

3 tablespoons granulated sugar

1 teaspoon pure vanilla extract

METHOD

1. In a large bowl, combine the cream, sugar, and vanilla. Using a wire whisk or an electric mixer, whip the cream until soft peaks appear. Watch it carefully as the cream continues to stiffen, and stop when it reaches the desired peak stage.

2. Use immediately or chill for up to 1 hour.

VARIATIONS

ALTERNATE SWEETENERS: You can use the recipe above using powdered sugar, brown sugar, honey, agave, or even artificial sweeteners. Add these slowly, as their potency differs.

CHOCOLATE CREAM: Melt 1 cup of chocolate in a microwave (in 15-second increments, stirring in between), then let cool until it's at room temperature, but still liquid. By hand, whisk the cooled chocolate into soft-peak whipped cream until just combined. Be careful, as the addition of chocolate makes ovewhipping easier.

COFFEE CREAM: By hand, whisk 1 tablespoon (or more, depending on your taste) of coffee extract into soft-peak sweetened whipped cream. You can also use 1 tablespoon instant espresso powder diluted in 1 tablespoon water.

COCONUT CREAM: Add ½ cup of canned coconut cream into soft-peak sweetened whipped cream and continue whipping until stiff. You can also pump up the coconut flavor by adding ½ teaspoon of coconut extract.

CITRUS CREAM: At the final stages of whipping your cream add the finely grated zest of a lemon, lime, or orange.

sabayon

MAKES ABOUT 3-4 CUPS

This is the same dessert as the Italian zabaglione. You can call it by either name, depending whether you are feeling more French or Italian on any given day. The Italian version classically uses Marsala for flavoring, but pastry chefs have long used the sabayon to add a foamy light component to composed desserts, usually with their own flavor additions, like calvados, reduced red wine syrups, champagne, or fruit purees. Make it your own by using any liquid flavoring in place of the brandy.

INGREDIENTS

½ cup heavy cream
4 egg yolks
½ cup sugar
2 tablespoons brandy

METHOD

1. Whip the cream to stiff peaks and set aside.

2. Fill a small saucepan with water and bring to a boil over high heat. When at the boil, reduce to a simmer. Combine the egg yolks, sugar, and brandy in a heatproof bowl, place over the steaming water in the saucepan, and begin whisking. Whisk continuously and vigorously until thick foamy ribbons form on the surface, and the color lightens to a pale yellow. Remove from the heat and continue whipping until cool.

3. Fold the whipped cream into cooled foamy egg yolk mixture. Serve immediately.

ganache

MAKES ABOUT 2 CUPS OF GANACHE

This classic recipe is the base of dozens of desserts. A friend of mine, and former colleague, pastry chef Sandy Teich, used to give a lecture called "The Miracle of Ganache." She nailed it with that title. Chilled and rolled into balls, it is the center of truffles. Poured hot over cakes, it is a glaze. Left at room temperature, it is an easy frosting and a delightful dessert topping. It can even be whipped to increase its lightness.

INGREDIENTS

1 cup heavy cream
8 ounces bittersweet chocolate, chopped
(or 1½ cups bittersweet chocolate chips)

METHOD

1. In a small saucepan, bring the cream to a boil over high heat.
2. Place the chocolate in a bowl. When at the boil, pour the hot cream over the chocolate. Let it sit for 3 minutes, then whisk lightly until smooth.

VARIATIONS

GLAZE: Make as-is and use immediately, poured over ice cream cakes, or used as a dip for your cones. (See page 127 for dipped cone—aka Brown Derby—how-to.)

ROOM TEMPERATURE: Let the ganache stand at room temperature for 1 to 2 hours until set and spreadable. It may take longer, depending on your climate, and up to overnight in a hot busy kitchen in the heat of the summer. So, this requires a bit of planning. Sorry.

WHIPPED: Use the room temperature variation and whip it like cream, but only as far as soft peak. Too far and it will look like chocolaty cottage cheese—better than regular cottage cheese, but not pretty.

MILK CHOCOLATE: Use milk chocolate instead of bittersweet, and adjust the measurements to 1 pound (16 ounces) of chocolate to 1 cup of cream.

WHITE CHOCOLATE: Use white chocolate instead of bittersweet, and adjust the measurements to 1½ pounds (24 ounces) of chocolate to 1 cup of cream.

SAUCES

Sauces can offer not only a nice textural difference and an enhanced flavor, but also an eye-catching embellishment to an otherwise plain presentation.

When choosing a sauce, keep in mind the overall composition of the plate. Avoid repetition (chocolate ice cream with chocolate cake) unless you are planning to make that your theme, as in a "medley of chocolate." Consider contrasts—pair sweet desserts with tart or tangy sauces, and vice versa. Pair creamy desserts with chunky sauces and compotes. Pair icy desserts with something smooth. This is the part of dessert creation that makes it art.

chocolate sauce

MAKES ABOUT 2 CUPS OF SAUCE

Chocolate sauce can be as easy as warming a ready-made ganache. But this sauce can be used hot or cold, and kept at the ready in the fridge for any late-night chocolate sauce emergency that might arise. Hey—you never know.

INGREDIENTS

2 tablespoons unsweetened cocoa powder
¾ cup water
½ cup sugar
Pinch of kosher salt
¼ cup corn syrup (light or dark)
4 ounces bittersweet chocolate, chopped or chips (about ¾ cup)

METHOD

1. Place the cocoa powder in a large bowl and set aside.
2. In a small saucepan, combine the water, sugar, salt, and corn syrup and bring to a boil over high heat. When at the boil, remove from the heat and slowly stir enough of the mixture into the cocoa powder to make a smooth paste. Add the remaining mixture, stirring, then add the chopped chocolate and stir until smooth.
3. Strain and use immediately, or store in the refrigerator for later use. This sauce can be used hot or cold.

hot fudge sauce

MAKES ABOUT 3 CUPS OF SAUCE

The difference between this and plain chocolate sauce is that the hot fudge will thicken when it hits cold ice cream. Its texture makes homey sundaes fun, but it's a little too gloppy for more refined plate decorations.

INGREDIENTS

8 ounces bittersweet chocolate, chopped or chips (about ½ cup)
6 tablespoons (3 ounces/¾ stick) unsalted butter

1½ cups water

1 cup sugar

½ cup corn syrup (light or dark)

1 teaspoon pure vanilla extract

1. Combine the chocolate and butter in a medium saucepan. Place over very low heat and stir continuously until melted.

2. Add the water, sugar, and corn syrup, increase the heat to a simmer, and continue stirring until well combined. Remove from the heat and add the vanilla. Use immediately, or cool and store in the refrigerator. To use it again rewarm it over a hot water bath, or slowly in the microwave, stirring every 15 to 20 seconds until melted.

white chocolate sauce

MAKES ABOUT 3 CUPS OF SAUCE

I usually find white chocolate too sweet. Here, the buttermilk and lemon juice help keep it all balanced.

INGREDIENTS

6 ounces white chocolate, chopped or chips (about 1 cup)

1 cup heavy cream

½ cup buttermilk

2 teaspoons pure vanilla extract

1 teaspoon fresh lemon juice

Pinch of salt

METHOD

1. Place the white chocolate in a large bowl.

2. In a saucepan, bring the cream to a boil and pour over the chopped white chocolate. Let sit for 3 minutes, then whisk until smooth.

3. Add the buttermilk, vanilla, lemon juice, and salt and whisk until smooth. The sauce is now ready to use.

VARIATIONS

Many additives can be used here, including liquids (extracts, coffee, liqueur, citrus juice), citrus zest, herbs,

and spices. Consider key lime–white chocolate, Kahlúa–white chocolate, pink peppercorn–white chocolate, or peppermint–white chocolate.

caramel sauce

MAKES ABOUT 3 CUPS OF SAUCE

This is a pastry must-have recipe. It will keep for weeks in the refrigerator, and can be embellished to suit your mood. (See Variations following.) Refer to pages 158–59 for information on cooking sugar if this is your first sugar rodeo.

INGREDIENTS

2 cups sugar

¼ cup water

1 tablespoon fresh lemon juice

1½ cups heavy cream

4 tablespoons (2 ounces/½ stick) unsalted butter

METHOD

1. In a large saucepan, combine the sugar and the water. Mix together well, wipe all stray sugar crystals off the inside of the pan, and place it over high heat. Cook, without moving or stirring.

2. When the mixture reaches a rolling boil, add the lemon juice to the center of the pot. Do not stir. Continue cooking until the sugar is dark, golden amber.

3. Immediately remove from the heat and carefully whisk in the cream. Be careful here. The cream will cause the caramel to explode like Mentos in Diet Coke. It might be prudent to wear an oven mitt while whisking. Once the bubbles have subsided, add the butter and whisk until smooth, then cool to room temperature.

VARIATIONS

FLAVORED CARAMEL: Any number of flavor additions can be made after the caramel sauce is complete. Try adding vanilla, citrus zest, orange liqueur, apple cider, champagne, balsamic vinegar, espresso, peanut butter, melted chocolate, or unsweetened coconut milk.

CLEAR CARAMEL GLAZE: For a totally different

look, add water or another clear liquid (coffee, brandy, vinegar, apple juice) in place of the cream. This makes a beautiful see-through sauce that allows you to feature floating flavor additives. It looks amazing with a vanilla bean, any ground spices (cinnamon, cardamom, black pepper), whole seeds (anise, fennel, sesame), flowers, tea leaves, coffee grounds—you name it. If you want a similar effect without the amber color, cook the syrup only as far as the hard-crack stage (see chart, page 159).

vanilla custard sauce
(crème anglaise)

MAKES ABOUT 4 CUPS SAUCE

Here it is. The classic custard that not only makes a nice sauce, but also is the base for traditional ice cream.

INGREDIENTS

3 cups milk
1 vanilla bean, split lengthwise and scraped, or 1 teaspoon pure vanilla extract
7 egg yolks
½ cup sugar

METHOD

1. If using vanilla bean, in a saucepan, bring the milk and vanilla bean to a simmer. Remove from the heat and let steep for 20 minutes. If using vanilla extract, bring the milk to a simmer and remove from the heat, and skip to step 4.
2. Place a medium bowl over another bowl of ice and set aside. Have ready a fine-mesh strainer, a whisk, and a rubber spatula.
3. Return the vanilla bean milk to a simmer over medium heat and remove the bean.
4. Meanwhile, combine the eggs and sugar in a small bowl and whisk together. Gradually add 1 cup of the warm vanilla milk to the eggs to temper, then pour the egg mixture back into the simmering milk in the

saucepan. Stir continuously, scraping the bottom of the pan and whisking to remove any lumps, until it thickens to the consistency of heavy cream.
5. Immediately strain the custard into the medium bowl and set atop the ice bath to cool. Stir occasionally for even and quicker cooling. Store the completely cooled sauce in the refrigerator.

VARIATIONS

FLAVORED: Like everything else in this book, the variations are limited only by your imagination. Flavoring crème anglaise should be done in the milk before the eggs are added. Steep the ingredients (herbs, spices, coffee, tea) in the milk, or stir them into the milk once it is warm (chocolate, pumpkin, peanut butter).

ENRICHED: Some chefs thicken their crème anglaise by replacing a portion of the milk with half-and-half or cream. My chefs always told me that was cheating, and that if I was good, I should be able to get the sauce thick enough with just milk. But over the years when using it for an ice cream base, I found that a little half-and-half made a creamier ice cream. For sauce, however, I obey the chef.

simple syrup

MAKES ABOUT 2 CUPS SYRUP

Sugar syrup does not sound like a particularly delicious sauce, and it isn't—until you add things to it. What it does offer is an interesting visual effect on a plate. A clear sauce with flavor elements suspended in it can be truly spectacular. Additions can include not only liquid flavorings (extract, liqueurs, juices, syrups, vinegars), but also coarsely ground spices (black or pink peppercorns, cinnamon, nutmeg, star anise, saffron threads), seeds (toasted white or black sesame, poppy seeds, fennel seeds), grated citrus zest, tiny leaves, a fine chiffonade of fresh herbs, or tiny petals from edible flowers. As always, be sure your flavors complement the rest of your dessert.

INGREDIENTS

2 cups sugar

2 cups water

METHOD

1. Combine the sugar and water in a large saucepan and bring to a boil over high heat. When at the boil, the syrup is done. If you'd like a little thicker syrup, continue boiling to evaporate some of the water, until the desired consistency is reached. (The syrup will get slightly thicker when it is cool.)

2. Remove from the heat, add the flavoring elements, then set it aside to steep and cool at room temperature.

FRUIT SAUCES

The list of fruit sauces is endless, but there are only two ways to make them—cooked or raw. Some fruits can be made into a sauce by simply pureeing them in a blender. Others benefit from cooking first, to soften the fibers, extract more liquids, deepen the color, and intensify the flavors. Some fruits can go either way, and others will be ruined if taken to the heat.

There are hundreds of recipes for fruit sauces out there with precise measurements. But I contend that they are all useless, because you never know how much sugar you will need. No matter how reliable your source, fruits never have a consistent amount of sweetness. The sugar level varies with the season, the variety, the degree of ripeness when harvested, and the amount of time it spends in your kitchen.

You should also consider the rest of your plate to determine how sweet you want your sauce. The only sure-fire way to make a great sauce is to taste the fruit, and add sugar slowly, tasting periodically until you reach the desired level of sweetness. Still, as I know such instructions make the more precision-oriented cooks cringe, I will advise you to start with a conservative ratio: 1 cup of fruit to 1 tablespoon of sugar or simple syrup.

I always add just a touch of salt and acid to fruit sauces, both cooked and raw, to bring out the natural fruit flavors. The sauce should never taste of acid or salt—it should taste like the perfectly ripe fruit itself. Flavorful additions are perfectly acceptable, and heartily encouraged. Liqueurs, spices, herbs, or even a blend of fruits can make a terrific dessert sauce.

FRESH/RAW FRUIT SAUCE

Sometimes referred to as a "coulis," a fresh, raw fruit sauce is as easy as it gets. Combine the fruit and simple syrup in a bar blender and puree until smooth. Add additional syrup as needed to taste. Add 3 to 4 drops of acid (lemon, lime, vinegar), and a pinch of salt, then pass the sauce through a fine-mesh strainer to remove residual fibers. Serve immediately, or store in the refrigerator.

BLENDERS

As I mentioned in the sorbet chapter, bar blenders are the best choice for making a puree. Their motion forces the food into the center blade for chopping. A food processor is not as efficient at this, because the centrifugal force sends the food to the outer edge of the bowl, away from the blade. But if a food processor is all you've got, just go for it. You can also just mash fruits through a strainer, like cooks did in the olden days.

COOKED FRUIT SAUCE

This method of sauce making is basically the same as the first, but the fruits are first cooked to release their juices, and to soften their textures. The sweeteners are best added during the cooking process, but the level of sweetness can be increased afterward using simple syrup in the blender if necessary. Additional flavors are best added during cooking so that their flavors can infuse.

Combine the fruit and sugar or simple syrup in a saucepan, and cook over medium heat stirring, until their liquids exude, and their pulp softens. Cool, puree, and strain.

Firmer fruits will benefit from a little butter in the pan first, a higher heat, and a quick sauté for caramelizing. See the chart below for which fruits should be sauced in which method.

Finally, some fruits can only be made into a sauce from juice form, and must simply be reduced until the required consistency is achieved. This method can also be used with wines, teas, soda pop, and vegetable juices (the sweetness of carrots and beets make them interesting dessert fodder.) Sweeten as necessary, add any infusions, place the juice in a large saucepan, and bring it to a boil. Keep the boil bubbling as much as possible, as it is the popping of the bubbles releasing the steam that causes the reduction. Test the mixture periodically by pouring a spoonful onto a plate to check its consistency. The sauce will be thicker as it cools.

fruit sauce cooking chart

	Raw Sauce	Cooked Sauce	Juice Reduction	Notes
APPLES		x		Sauté with butter and sugar until soft and caramelized before pureeing. Thin with apple juice.
AVOCADO	x			Yes, this is a fruit, and used as such in much of the world. Thin it down with cream and simple syrup for a rich smooth accompaniment to tropical flavors.
BANANAS		x		If you pureed these raw, they would turn brown. Sauté with butter and brown sugar until caramelized. Then puree, thinning with simple syrup, juice, or rum.
BERRIES	x	x	x	Berry sauces are more intense when cooked. Combine in a saucepan with sugar, lemon juice, zest, and a pinch of salt, and cook until juicy.
CITRUS		x	x	Reduce the juices, or cook like a marmalade. Slice rind and all, add sugar, and cook until tender and juicy. Then puree and strain.

(continued)

	Raw Sauce	Cooked Sauce	Juice Reduction	Notes
DRAGON FRUIT		x		This tastes like a kiwi-pear hybrid when ripe. If not fully ripened, it will benefit from the addition of another fruit, such as berries, citrus, or tropicals.
FIG		x		Chop, skin and all, and cook like a jam, with sugar, lemon juice, zest, and a pinch of salt, stirring until the flesh is softened and juicy, then puree and strain.
GRAPES			x	Reduce store-bought grape juice, or puree fresh grapes, strain off the juice, then reduce.
GUAVA	x			Most places only get guava in paste form, which needs to be warmed and diluted. But the fresh fruit can be simply pureed, sweetened, and strained.
LOQUAT		x		Remove the pits and cook like a jam, with sugar, orange or lemon zest, and a pinch of salt. When soft and juicy, puree, then strain the skins, and thin if necessary with juice or simple syrup.
MANGO	x	x		Cooked or raw, the mango will benefit from lime juice and zest. Often no sugar is required, so taste the fruit first.
MELONS	x			Cooked melons taste bad and look ugly! The water separates out and the entire thing looks broken and weird. Just puree them raw. Like the mango, sometimes no sugar is needed, but lime is always appreciated.
PASSION FRUIT	x			Best raw, but difficult to access. Ripe skin is wrinkly and dark. Scoop out contents into a fine-mesh strainer and press through to separate the seeds, which are edible, but unremarkable. Some chefs like the look, in which case, add back only a few seeds.

	Raw Sauce	Cooked Sauce	Juice Reduction	Notes
PEARS		x		Cook in the same manner as apples (above) or poach in liquid (wine, cider, spiced syrup) before pureeing.
PERSIMMONS		x		Fuyus should be sautéed like apples, while the Hachiyas are better cooked as berries would be, like a jam.
PINEAPPLE	x	x		Perfectly ripe, they can be used raw. But most of the pineapple we get on the mainland is not ripe yet, and will benefit from a sauté in butter or oil with a little sugar, until caramelized and tender.
POMEGRANATE			x	Juicing is the only game in town for the pom—but the addition of some whole seeds makes a lovely presentation.
PRICKLY PEAR		x		Cook to soften the pulp of this exotic magenta fruit, then puree and strain out the seeds. Sweetness is highly variable, and it benefits from lime.
QUINCE		x		This is only edible when cooked. Sautéing is possible, but more traditionally the fruit is poached in infused water or juice until tender and rosy-colored.
STONE FRUITS		x		Cook either as a jam, with sugar, lemon juice and zest, and salt, or sauté in butter and sugar until caramelized. The jam method is a bit fresher-tasting, the sauté deeper and richer.
TOMATO		x		Yep, it's a fruit, and is treated as such in some parts of the world. The French make a caramelized tomato sauce that is to die for. Sauté ripe slices in butter and sugar until caramelized and tender. Then puree or leave chunky (mmm) and serve with vanilla ice cream.

FRUIT COMPOTES

Fruit compotes are nothing more than chunky sauces. They can be raw, cooked, or a combination of the two. A compote is an excellent way to add texture to a dessert, and can be served warm to add a contrasting temperature.

The best compotes use a variety of similar or complementary fruits, and have been stewed or macerated with other seasonings (liqueurs, juices, herbs, spices, zest). Use the fruit sauce chart (page 139–41) as your guide to getting your compote started. Fruits that are best used fresh can be added raw at later stages of a compote for added texture. The following are a couple of my favorite compote recipes. Use them as a jumping-off point for creating your own saucy accompaniments.

mixed berry compote with opal basil

MAKES ABOUT 3 CUPS OF COMPOTE

INGREDIENTS

1 pint raspberries

1 pint blackberries

1 pint blueberries

Finely grated zest of 1 lemon

½ teaspoon fresh lemon juice

¼ cup chopped opal basil (plus 5 to 6 large leaves, reserved for garnish)

¼ cup sugar

2 tablespoons Pernod (or Sambuca, ouzo, arak, anisette)

METHOD

1. Combine half a pint of each of the berries in a small saucepan. Add the lemon zest, juice, basil, and sugar. Set over medium heat and cook, stirring, until the berries are juicy and jammy. Remove from the heat, add the remaining berries and anise-flavored liqueur, then cool. Serve hot or cold.

VARIATIONS

STONE FRUITS: Use the same method with peaches, nectarines, or cherries. Try adding sage with plums, and some thyme with apricots.

CRANBERRIES: These tart berries must be cooked, which is perfect for compotes. Cook a cup of cranberries, then add to it another fresh berry when the crans cool.

winter fruit compote

MAKES ABOUT 3 CUPS OF COMPOTE

Use your favorite fruit. I have listed mine, but it will work fine with whatever variety of apple and pear you prefer, and with any dried fruit or cooked chunks of winter squash.

INGREDIENTS

¼ cup dried currants

¼ cup dried apricots, chopped

¼ cup golden raisins

¼ cup dried cherries

Finely grated zest and juice of 1 orange

¼ cup Grand Marnier

1 cinnamon stick

1 cup boiling water, or as needed

2 tablespoons (1 ounce) unsalted butter

2 Fuji apples, peeled, cored, and sliced

2 Anjou pears, peeled, cored, and sliced

¼ cup packed brown sugar

1 teaspoon ground cardamom

½ vanilla bean, split and scraped

METHOD

1. In a large container, combine the dried fruits, orange zest and juice, Grand Marnier, and cinnamon stick. Add boiling water until the fruits are submerged. Set aside at room temperature.

2. Melt the butter in a large saucepan. Add the apple and pear slices, sugar, and cardamom and sauté until soft and caramelized. Remove from the heat and add

to the dried fruits. Add the vanilla bean and stir the mixture briefly.

3. Let the mixture macerate for at least an hour, but longer if possible, and up to several days for maximum deliciousness. Remove the vanilla bean. Serve warm or at room temperature.

tropical fruit salsa

MAKES ABOUT 4 CUPS OF SALSA

The size dice you choose is up to you, but the smaller the pieces, the more elegant the finished salsa—and the less it looks like a fruit salad!

INGREDIENTS

1 cup fresh ripe pineapple, diced
1 cup mango, diced
1 cup papaya, diced
1 kiwi fruit, diced
Finely grated zest and juice of 1 lime
¼ cup pomegranate seeds
¼ cup chiffonade of fresh mint
¼ cup simple syrup
1 teaspoon orange flower water
Pinch of kosher salt

FRUIT SALSA

This is nothing but a glorified fruit salad. But by cutting the fruit into a smaller dice, it makes an amazing dessert element. I have provided a tropical version but this works well with any fruit combination. Try it with berries, stone fruits, or suprêmes of citrus. Use only one type of fruit (as in a citrus salsa), or combine them, as I did in the above recipe. Anything goes! The caveat is that they need to be fruits that are good raw, and they need to be ripe.

METHOD

1. Combine all the ingredients in a large bowl. Toss and set aside at room temperature to macerate for 1 hour.
2. Serve at room temperature, or refrigerate.

lemon curd

MAKES ABOUT 1 QUART OF CURD

Though not technically a sauce, curd can be a useful addition to a dessert plate composition. It is tangy and creamy, it can be thickened with the addition of whipped cream or meringue, or thinned by water or juice, or limoncello to make a sauce.

INGREDIENTS

6 whole large eggs
5 large egg yolks
1¾ cups sugar
Finely grated zest of 4 lemons
$1^1/_3$ cups fresh lemon juice
16 tablespoons (8 ounces/2 sticks) unsalted butter
Pinch of salt

METHOD

1. Combine the whole eggs, egg yolks, sugar, lemon zest, lemon juice, butter, and salt in a large saucepan. Stir together and place over high heat. Cook, stirring continuously, until the mixture thickens to a sour cream-like consistency, about 5 minutes.
2. Remove from the heat and immediately pass through a fine-mesh strainer to remove any eggy bits. Cover with plastic wrap pressed directly on the surface of the curd to prevent a skin from forming as it cools. Cool and store refrigerated.

VARIATIONS

LIME CURD: Easy-peasy. Just replace the lemon zest and juice with lime zest and juice.

OTHER FRUIT: Most fruits do not contain the acid required to thicken curd. So variations with less acidic fruits need at least ¼ cup of lemon or lime juice. When making orange curd, grapefruit curd, cranberry curd, pomegranate curd, and passion fruit curd, use this ratio in the given recipe: $2/3$ cup other juice, $1/3$ cup lemon or lime juice.

AS A PIE FILLING: In case you were unaware, curd is often used as the base of lemon pies and tarts. If you want to use it as such, you must have your shell ready to go so that the curd can be poured directly from the pan, through a strainer, and into the shell. If it doesn't cool in the shape of the pie, the slices will not hold their shape.

CANDIES

If you think of candy in terms of your childhood, it does not initially seem like a classy dessert element. But if you can harness its crunchy shine, a simple small candied element can totally class up the joint. (Be sure to read the short section on sugar, pages 158–59.)

candied nuts

MAKES ABOUT 2 CUPS OF NUTS

These nuts add a rich toasty crunch to your plated desserts. Use any nut you like to create these delightfully golden nuggets, but keep them whole, not chopped.

INGREDIENTS

2 cups nuts
2 cups sugar
1 cup water
1 tablespoon fresh lemon juice

METHOD

1. Preheat the oven to 375°F. Have at the ready a fine-mesh strainer, a large metal spoon, 2 large saucepans, and a large sheet of parchment or waxed paper, coated with nonstick cooking spray.
2. Spread the nuts out on a rimmed baking sheet and toast until golden brown and fragrant, 5 to 10 minutes. Keep warm.

3. Meanwhile, combine the sugar and water in a large saucepan. Mix to moisten all the sugar, and wipe any stray sugar granules off the inside of the pot. Place gently over high heat and cook, without stirring, until the sugar reaches a golden amber caramel stage (325° to 345°F).
4. Remove from the heat and let stand for 2 minutes until the bubbles subside and the mixture thickens slightly. (It will continue to cook slightly, and may turn darker, which is normal and fine.)
5. Pour the warm toasted nuts into the pan with the sugar mixture, stir quickly, then immediately pour the mixture with the nuts through a fine-mesh strainer, letting excess sugar mixture drain into the second saucepan. Immediately spread the caramel-coated nuts on the prepared parchment paper, separating them from each other as much as possible. Set aside to cool.
6. Break the cooled nuts into pieces as individual as possible. Store airtight at room temperature for a day or two, or freeze airtight for long-term storage.

VARIATIONS

NUT TEAR DROPS: Using a long skewer, spear each whole nut individually like a nut pop. Make caramelized sugar, as above. After the sugar has caramelized and rested for a few minutes, let it sit until it has thickened to corn syrup consistency, about 5 minutes more. Dip each skewered nut into the caramel, so that it makes a long drip, then suspend the nut so the drip can cool and harden. Use as a garnish with the long drip facing up.

BRITTLE SHEETS: Rather than strain the excess sugar out as in the main recipe, pour it all out with the nuts onto the prepared parchment and spread out as thinly as possible. Allow it to cool, then break it into shards.

brown sugar–candied nuts

MAKES ABOUT 2 CUPS OF NUTS

This recipe may sound similar to the caramelized nuts above, but the end product is very different. The process is a little faster and easier than the caramelized sugar version, and it enables you to add another flavor element. It's not ideal for every dessert, but it makes a great mix-in, and it's not a bad bar snack, either.

INGREDIENTS

2 cups nuts

⅓ cup packed brown sugar

1 teaspoon kosher salt

½ teaspoon spice (cinnamon, cayenne pepper, orange zest, black pepper, anise seed, sesame seeds, ginger, nutmeg, etc.) (optional)

3 tablespoons (1½ ounces) unsalted butter

METHOD

1. In a small bowl, toss together the nuts, sugar, salt, and any spice if using. Be sure the nuts are well coated. Coat a rimmed baking sheet with nonstick cooking spray and set aside.

2. Melt the butter in a large sauté pan over high heat. When the butter has melted, add the coated nuts and cook, stirring constantly, for 3 to 5 minutes until the sugar has melted and the nuts are toasted. Pour them immediately out onto the prepared baking sheet, spread out into a single layer, and cool completely.

peanut brittle

MAKES ABOUT 1 POUND OF BRITTLE

This timeless (another word for old-fashioned) recipe from the world of candy making might seem boring, but consider this: No one said you have to use peanuts. Try it with walnuts, hazelnuts, pine nuts, pumpkin seeds, or cashews (gesundheit). Or add some spice at the end for an added punch! Not everything old is boring. (I am living proof.)

INGREDIENTS

1 cup sugar

½ cup corn syrup

1½ cups nuts

1 tablespoon (½ ounce) unsalted butter

1½ teaspoons baking soda

1 teaspoon pure vanilla extract

METHOD

1. Spread a large sheet of parchment or waxed paper out on your counter and coat it with nonstick cooking spray. Have nearby an offset metal spatula, also coated with spray.

2. Combine the sugar, corn syrup, nuts, and butter in a large saucepan and cook over high heat until the mixture begins to boil. Stir occasionally, and continue cooking until it reaches the hard-crack stage (300°F). (See chart, page 159.)

3. Immediately remove from the heat, add the baking soda and vanilla together, and stir them in. The mixture will bubble up like lava, so be careful. As soon as the mixture is completely foamy, pour it out onto the prepared paper.

4. Spread the candy as thinly as possible using the prepared spatula. Let cool completely before breaking apart in shards. Store the finished, cooled candy airtight at room temperature, or freeze in ziptop plastic bags for prolonged storage.

VARIATIONS

ANOTHER NUT: As stated in the headnote of this recipe, any nut will work, or any seed. Consider the meal you are cooking, the season, the event, and choose accordingly.

SPICE BRITTLE: Add the spices of your choice to this recipe with the baking soda and vanilla. Try cinnamon, black, white or pink pepper, cayenne pepper, cardamom, anise, or fennel seeds.

brown sugar toffee

MAKES ABOUT 1 POUND OF TOFFEE

Toffee is a great ice cream add-in, and a great crunchy dessert element. It also makes a delightful midnight sugar fix. Consider preparing for such an occasion by hiding a bag in the freezer behind the frozen peas.

INGREDIENTS

1¼ cups packed brown sugar

2 tablespoons water

8 tablespoons (4 ounces/1 stick) unsalted butter

¼ teaspoon baking soda

1 teaspoon pure vanilla extract

6 ounces bittersweet chocolate, chopped (or 1 cup bittersweet chocolate chips)

1 cup chopped nuts

METHOD

1. Spread a large sheet of parchment or waxed paper out onto your counter and coat it with nonstick cooking spray. Have nearby an offset metal spatula, also coated with spray.

2. Combine the brown sugar, water, and butter in a large saucepan and bring to a boil over high heat. Stirring occasionally, continue cooking to hard-crack stage (285°F). (See chart, page 159.)

3. Immediately remove from the heat, add the baking soda and vanilla together, and stir them in until the mixture is foamy. Immediately pour out onto the prepared paper and spread as thinly as possible. Work fast! The candy cools quickly!

4. Sprinkle the toffee with chocolate and let it stand for 5 minutes. When the chocolate has melted, spread it out thinly to cover the toffee, then sprinkle it with the chopped nuts. Chill just until the chocolate has set, then break it into shards. Store the finished, cooled candy airtight at room temperature, or freeze in ziptop plastic bags for prolonged storage (and snacks).

VARIATION

CHOCOLATE-NUT COMBOS: Any type of nut and chocolate will work on top of this toffee. Try dark chocolate and toasted pecans, white chocolate and macadamia nuts, or milk chocolate and hazelnuts. If you use milk chocolate and almonds it tastes jut like Almond Roca. And at Christmas be sure to make this with dark chocolate and crushed candy canes.

candied citrus zest

MAKES ABOUT ½ CUP OF CANDIED CITRUS ZEST

You have to pay top dollar for this item in the stores—if you can find it. And here's a secret: the store-bought version is nowhere near as good as when it's homemade. Plus, it's cheap, easy, and impressive. You can cut the zest in big hunks or long ribbons, but be sure to keep it about ½ inch thick, and leave some of the pith attached. One last tip—superchefs repeat the first blanching step two or three times. It improves the flavor and increases tenderness.

INGREDIENTS

4 cups water

½ cup citrus peel strips

1 cup sugar

METHOD

1. Bring 3 cups of water to boil in a small saucepan. Add the peel and blanch for 1 minute. This removes the bitter oils. Strain out the peel and discard the water.

2. In the same pot, combine the sugar with the remaining 1 cup water and bring to a boil over high heat. Add the blanched peel, reduce the heat to a bare simmer, and cook until tender and translucent, 30 to 60 minutes.

3. Drain off the syrup (and reserve for a delicious sauce), and spread the peels out on a baking sheet or parchment to cool and dry. When cool, toss the peels in granulated sugar. Store airtight at room temperature, or in the freezer for extended periods.

VARIATIONS

CARROTS: You can make some nifty carrot ribbons with this method. Peel off the carrot in thick lengthwise strips with a potato peeler, then follow the directions above. Carrots usually cook faster, so check them after 10 minutes.

GINGER: Candied ginger not only makes a great garnish, but also a great mix-in. Slice the ginger in thin coins, or shave in thin lengthwise strips, and follow the directions above. For a mix-in, dice the finished product.

APPLE CHIPS: Slice the apples thin in cross sections, so each slice has a piece of the core in the middle, like a flower. Omit the blanching, but cook in simple syrup until translucent. Drain, and lay each slice out on a baking sheet lined with parchment paper. Top with a second sheet of paper and bake at 325°F until dry, about 30 minutes. (The second paper weighs the fruit down a bit, and prevents excessive curling.)

PINEAPPLE FLOWERS: Use the apple method for pineapple. The resulting garnish looks like pretty flowers, hence the name.

sesame candies

MAKES ABOUT 2 CUPS OF CANDY

These are pretty easy candies, but they look very fancy and complicated. I won't tell if you won't.

INGREDIENTS

2 cups sesame seeds
¼ teaspoon ground cinnamon
¼ teaspoon ground ginger
Pinch of salt
½ cup honey
½ cup packed brown sugar

METHOD

1. Line a small cake pan with aluminum foil. Coat it with cooking spray, then set it aside.
2. Toast the sesame seeds in a dry skillet, stirring, until golden and fragrant, 30 to 60 seconds. Immediately pour out of the pan into a large bowl to stop the cooking. Add the cinnamon, ginger, and salt.
3. In a small saucepan, combine the honey and sugar and bring it to a boil. Cook for 1 minute, then pour immediately over seeds. Stir together and transfer to the prepared pans. Press the seeds flat, then cool for 5 minutes before cutting into the desired shapes.

SCHMANCY GARNISHING

Fancily shaped cookies, like tuiles and nut lace, can elevate your ice cream from backyard snacking to white tablecloth dining. Of course, there is nothing to keep you from enjoying your tuiles in the backyard, too.

tuiles

MAKES ABOUT 3 CUPS OF TUILE BATTER

This thin wafer cookie gets its name from terra-cotta roof tiles (which were manufactured in, among other places, Paris, at the site of the current Tuileries Garden). They take a little practice, but once you get the hang of them, there is little you can't make with them. The classic shape was the tile—somewhat "Pringles"-shaped. You also see them as a rolled "cigarette." (Think Pepperidge Farm Pirouette cookies.) The key to success is using a nonstick silicone mat on your baking sheet. It keeps the cookie from sticking, and makes them easy to manipulate when hot.

INGREDIENTS

1 cup powdered sugar, sifted
¾ cup all-purpose flour, sifted
3 egg whites
8 tablespoons (4 ounces/1 stick) unsalted butter, melted and cooled

METHOD

1. Combine the sugar, flour, and egg whites in a bowl and mix together to form a paste. Slowly add the melted butter and continue to mix until smooth.
2. Chill the batter for at least 30 minutes (or overnight) before baking.
3. Preheat the oven to 375°F. Line a baking sheet with a silicone mat. Use a stencil to spread batter in thin sheets on the mat into the desired shapes.
4. Bake for 3 to 5 minutes, just until brown around the edges. Remove from the oven and immediately remove from the pan and form. Work quickly, as they cool into a crisp, rigid wafer. Be warned—they're hot! Tuiles can also be left flat, if you desire.

CHOCOLATE TUILE: Substitute 2 tablespoons of cocoa powder for 2 tablespoons of flour.

SPICED AND SEASONED TUILE: Fold any spices you like into the finished batter. Consider lemon zest and black pepper, white pepper and ginger, orange zest and cayenne, anise seeds and vanilla bean, toasted coconut and lime zest, or sesame seeds and green tea powder. Really, the options are endless.

parmesan tuiles

MAKES ABOUT 4 TO 8 TUILES

These are related to the tuiles above only in name and the use of the silicone mat. They make a great salty garnish, for both sweet and savory applications.

INGREDIENT

1 cup grated Parmesan cheese

METHOD

1. Preheat the oven to 375°F. Line a baking sheet with a silicone mat. Mat-less cooks can coat the baking sheet with nonstick cooking spray and a thin dusting of flour.

2. Using a tablespoon, place mounds of the cheese on the silicone mat, leaving 2 inches of space in between. Bake until melted, spread, and browned.

3. Cool flat, or remove from the silicone mat with an offset spatula and drape over a wooden spoon handle or rolling pin to set a curve.

nut lace cookies

MAKES ABOUT 2 CUPS BATTER

These wafers are formed the same way as the tuiles, but they take a little longer to cook. This recipe uses almonds, but there is no reason you can't substitute another nut, seed, or coconut. You can even leave it nut-free.

INGREDIENTS

1¾ cups powdered sugar, sifted
¼ cup all-purpose flour, sifted
6 tablespoons (3 ounces/¾ stick) unsalted butter, melted and cooled
1¾ cups sliced almonds
Finely grated zest and juice of 1 orange
1 tablespoon Grand Marnier (or another orange liqueur, or an extract)

METHOD

1. Combine the sugar and flour in a bowl, and slowly stir in the butter to form a paste. Add the almonds, orange zest and juice, and Grand Marnier and mix until smooth.

2. Preheat the oven to 350°F. Line a baking sheet with a silicone mat. Drop small spoonfuls of batter onto the mat and spread with an offset metal spatula into the desired shapes, leaving at least 2 inches between cookies.

3. Bake for 5 to 6 minutes until golden brown. Cool until the cookie can be removed in one piece. Serve as flat wafers, or shape when warm, as with tuiles.

SHAPING TUILE

The easiest way to make your tuile shapes is with a stencil. I make my own out of recycled plastic lids, because they can be washed and reused. The lids are great because they are the exact thickness I need and make spreading my batter uniformly a snap. A small offset metal spatula will prove invaluable here, both for spreading the batter, and for manipulating the hot cookie. For a bowl, invert a glass as a template to drape the hot round tuile over. For a taco, drape the cookie over the handle of a wooden spoon. You will have breakage, so be prepared. It's almost impossible to make a batch of tuiles without breaking any. But save the broken bits! Crunched up, folded into ganache, and rolled into truffles, they taste just like a crunch bar!

additional recipe
variations

〰〰〰

ice creams

Mint Chip (page 24)

CANDY CANE: Replace the mint extract with vanilla, omit the food coloring, and fold in 1 cup of crushed candy canes along with the chocolate.

CHOCOLATE-RASPBERRY-MINT: This is a luscious trifecta of deliciousness. Toss 1 cup of raspberries in 1 tablespoon of granulated sugar and the finely grated zest of 1 lemon. Set it aside for 1 hour or more to macerate. The raspberries will intensify in flavor and exude some water. Omit the food coloring from the master recipe, then give the berries a rough smash before folding them into the base before the cream goes in.

ORANGE-PEPPERMINT: In ye olden days, thick porous peppermint sticks were sold with oranges, into which they were inserted to suck out the juice. Revisit this flavor memory by adding the finely grated zest of 2 oranges to the recipe above. Definitely omit the food coloring, as the zest will give the base a lovely orange hue. This flavor pair works well with or without the chocolate chips, and with fresh chopped spearmint in place of the candies.

Summer Berry (page 40)

BLACKBERRY-JUNIPER: Juniper is most recognizable as the flavor of gin, but its heady aromatics are a surprisingly attractive pair with sweet-tart berries, especially blackberries. Crush 2 to 3 whole berries and steep them in the cup of milk, warmed for 30 to 60 seconds in the microwave. Let it cool completely before straining off the juniper and proceeding with the master recipe as directed.

FRAISES DE BOIS: These tiny strawberries are fairly uncommon in the United States, but they occasionally show up at farmers' markets for a week or two in the summer. When they do appear, grab them and use them in this recipe. Remember to save some pretty ones for garnish.

PLUM-SAGE: Slice thinly 4 sweet, ripe plums (any variety), and combine them in the saucepan as in the master recipe with the addition of ¼ cup of chopped fresh sage leaves. This is one of my favorite pairs ever!

Cherry-Chocolate (page 42)

DRIED CHERRIES: If you can't get fresh cherries, try this combo with dried cherries. Simply macerate the dried cherries in the kirschwasser, adding a little hot water until the dried fruit is submerged. Let them soak until they are plumped, then drain off the excess liquid. Add an additional tablespoon of lemon juice to the base, as it will have been drained off here. Top this version with some toasted almonds.

CRISS-CROSS: Omit the melted chocolate. Puree the macerated cherries and fold them into the base before the cream is folded in. Then add chopped chocolate as a swirl-in—same flavors, different texture.

RASPBERRY-CHOCOLATE: Make the master recipe with raspberries instead of cherries. Omit the kirschwasser, and use brandy, Chambord, or vanilla instead.

CHERRY-ALMOND: For this classic combination, omit the chocolate, and replace the milk with almond milk. For added texture, stir in some toasted, sliced almonds before the cream is folded into the mixture.

Peach (page 44)

NECTARINE: The nectarine is nothing but a peach without fuzz. Really! They were bred that way. So just follow the same recipe, and change the name.

APRICOT: As with the nectarine variation, simply substitute apricots for the peaches. Use about 3 cups sliced apricots to equal 3 large peaches. I like to make apricot ice cream with the addition of ½ of a scraped vanilla bean, and a tablespoon of amaretto.

GINGER PEACHY: Ginger and peaches were born to be together. Add a pinch of ground ginger with the nutmeg, then fold in chopped candied ginger with the whipped cream.

PEACH-PECAN: A southern classic. Fold in chopped toasted pecans with the whipped cream. (Read about properly toasted nuts on page 33.) Up the ante by folding in chopped pecan pralines!

Pineapple-Pepper (page 46)

PINEAPPLE-RUM: Add 2 tablespoons of dark rum (such as Myers's) to the base before the whipped cream is folded in. You can leave the peppercorns in, or take them out—both ways work with rum. You might also go the piña colada route, and replace the milk with coconut milk.

PINEAPPLE-SAGE: This earthy herb is given new life against tropical fruits. Omit the pepper, and add ½ cup of chopped fresh sage to the pineapple as it sautés, and continue with the recipe as directed.

PINEAPPLE UPSIDE-DOWN CAKE: For a flavor reminiscent of this mid-century favorite, increase the molasses to 2 tablespoons, omit the pepper, and fold in ½ cup of chopped maraschino cherries with the whipped cream.

PINEAPPLE–BLUE CHEESE: The key to this pair is subtlety. Omit the molasses and peppers, then stir in ½ cup Stilton or Maytag blue cheese to the sautéed pineapple as it sits cooling. Proceed with the recipe as directed, and serve with buttery shortbread or chopped toasted walnuts.

Lavender (page 48)

LAVENDER-BLACKBERRY: Macerate a pint of fresh, ripe blackberries with 1 teaspoon of sugar for an hour. Add the exuded juice to the lavender base before folding in the cream, then layer the ice cream in the freezer container with the berries.

APRICOT-LAVENDER: Increase the lavender to ¼ cup. Sauté 2 cups of sliced ripe apricots in 1 tablespoon of butter and 1 teaspoon of sugar until softened and caramelized. Cool completely, then stir into the base before the whipped cream is folded in.

Orange Flower Water–Almond (page 50)

ORANGE FLOWER–JUNIPER: Orange flower water is an ingredient in gin or Ramos fizz cocktails. Re-create this delightful old-timey flavor by replacing the almond milk with regular milk, and add to it 2 to 3 crushed juniper berries. Warm the milk in the microwave for 30 to 60 seconds, then set aside to steep and cool completely. When cool, drain off the juniper berries and proceed with the recipe as directed. Top with a shot of Tanqueray, or use it in a tonic water float.

Key Lime (page 51)

WHITE CHOCOLATE–LIME: The key lime is the perfect fruit to tame über-rich and sweet white chocolate. Melt 1 cup of white chocolate chips or chunks in the microwave for 30 to 60 seconds, stirring intermittently. Slowly stir in the 1 cup of milk, then add this to the juice and sweetened condensed milk base and proceed with the recipe as directed.

Peppermint Stick Crunch (page 53)

CHOCOLATE-PEPPERMINT: This is a classic pair, and there are several ways to combine them with this ice cream. You can make a swirl by layering the ice cream base, peppermints, and ganache as you pack it for the freezer. You can fold in chocolate chips or chunks as you fold in the whipped cream. You can even layer the ice cream with a separate chocolate ice cream for a marbled effect.

ORANGE-PEPPERMINT: This classic old-timey treat (which you can read about on page 149) can be re-created easily here by adding the zest of 2 large oranges to the milk as it warms with the peppermints.

PEPPERMINT-MOCHA: A million Starbucks customers can't be wrong. Add 2 tablespoons of instant coffee or espresso powder and ¼ cup chocolate chips to the warming peppermint milk and stir until the chocolate has melted, then proceed with the recipe as directed.

WHITE CHOCOLATE-PEPPERMINT: Layer ½ cup of chopped white chocolate or mini chips as you layer the peppermint sticks.

Meyer Lemon (page 54)

LEMON-LAVENDER: Add 2 tablespoons of crushed lavender buds to the cup of milk and warm together in the microwave for 30 to 60 seconds. Set aside to steep and cool, then proceed with the recipe as directed.

Pumpkin (page 56)

PUMPKIN-AMARETTO: Pumpkin raviolis topped with crushed amaretti cookies and browned sage butter are a regular menu item in both the Lombardy and Emilia-Romagna regions of Italy. It might surprise you to find that, as an ice cream, these flavors really spring to life, too. Sauté ¼ cup of chopped fresh sage and ¼ cup of crushed sliced almonds in a tablespoon of butter until the herbs, nuts, and butter begin to brown. Remove from the heat and cool completely, then stir together with the pumpkin. Omit all the spices from the master recipe with the exception of the nutmeg, and proceed with the recipe as directed.

PUMPKIN-GINGER: Ginger is a frequent addition to pumpkin pie spice blend. But it is often overlooked as a featured flavor. Omit the spices from the above recipe, and replace them with ½ teaspoon of ground ginger. Then finely chop ½ cup of candied ginger and fold it into the base with the whipped cream.

CHUNKY PUMPKIN: If you are a fan of roasted pumpkin, dice and roast 3 cups with a little butter and salt until tender. Make the vanilla ice cream base on page 12, and fold in the roasted pumpkin and the above spice mix (for pumpkin-ginger) with the whipped cream. It's the same idea, with a little different textural take.

Caramel (page 60)

CARAMEL–BLACK PEPPER: Hot and sweet are an international favorite. Stir in ½ to 1 teaspoon of freshly cracked black peppercorns or pink peppercorns to the caramel base before the whipped cream is folded in. If you are adventurous, you might also try adding red chile flakes, or a tablespoon of chile paste made from dried pasilla or New Mexico chiles.

Honey-Kumquat (page 68)

CITRON: A lemony citrus fruit that is mostly zest, the citron can be bought fresh, or already candied. If you use it fresh, simply exchange it for the kumquats in the recipe, dicing them (whole) into smaller-than-bite-size pieces. If you use the candied variety, omit the blanching and honey poaching, and just stir them into the milk base with the zest of 1 fresh lemon.

BUDDHA'S HAND: This odd and ancient citrus fruit has started popping up in farmers' markets here and there during the winter season. Chop it into a small dice and proceed as directed. To accentuate the lemony flavor, replace the honey with plain granulated sugar, and omit the orange flower water. If you want to, a hint of anise (toasted seeds, star anise, or in the form of liqueur) provides a lovely accent.

KAFFIR LIME, COCONUT, AND GINGER: Another citrus fruit that is more skin than pulp, the kaffir lime is more often used for its fragrant leaves in curries and soups. Use this chopped zest in place of the kumquats, add some fresh grated ginger instead of the orange flower water, and substitute canned unsweetened coconut milk for the regular milk.

Sweet Potato–Marshmallow Swirl (page 70)

SWEET POTATO–CARAMEL PECAN STREUSEL: Replacing the fluff with caramel-pecan streusel is delicious, as is dried fruit compote, and even straight chocolate or white chocolate ganache.

REAL YAM: If you are lucky enough to live in a place that sells real yams, by all means, use them! The purple ones will make the most striking product.

Cardamon (page 74)

WINTER SPICE BLEND: Cardamom isn't the only spice that evokes winter. Make your own blend to suit your preferences, using any or all of the following: cinnamon, nutmeg, allspice, anise, ginger, and cloves. Don't add too much clove, though, as it can make your tongue go numb.

ANISE SEED: Anise is a favorite great international flavor that you can get by using crushed anise or fennel seeds, toasted briefly in a dry skillet before adding into the milk. Try topping this version with a shot of anise liqueur (Sambuca, ouzo, arak, Pernod) or a sprinkling of mukhwas, the Indian after-dinner candy-spice blend with candy-coated fennel seeds.

APPLE-CARDAMOM: Sauté 3 peeled, cored, and sliced apples in 2 tablespoons each of butter and sugar. When they are caramelized, add ½ cup of water and cook until tender. Cool completely, then puree the apples and add them to the ice cream base before the whipped cream is folded in. Replace ¼ cup of the milk with ¼ cup sour cream. Try the same method with pears or bananas.

COCONUT, CARDAMOM, AND SAFFRON: For an exotic twist on this recipe, replace the milk with canned unsweetened coconut milk, and add 2 to 3 threads of saffron that have been toasted briefly in a dry skillet and crushed into the steep. Complete this idea with some really ripe sliced mango.

Hazelnut (page 76)

HAZELNUT-ORANGE: Add the zest of 2 oranges and ½ teaspoon of orange flower water to the base before folding in the whipped cream.

ANOTHER NUT: The same technique will work for any other nut—walnuts, cashews, almonds, and of course, peanuts. Then try your hand at walnut–black-pepper, cashew-ginger, and peanut-sesame by adding in the extra flavors to the base before folding in the whipped cream.

gelatos

Gianduja (page 81)

NO GIANDUJA?: If you have trouble finding gianduja in your area, there are several options. You can substitute 8 ounces of finely chopped milk chocolate and 4 ounces of hazelnut paste. Hazelnut paste, though, might be a harder find than the gianduja. If that is the case, you can toast whole hazelnuts and run them warm through a food processor to create your own hazelnut paste. (See the recipe for Hazelnut Ice Cream, page 76). You can also use Nutella, with the addition of 4 ounces of milk chocolate, as gianduja is a more chocolaty product.

HAZELNUT-PRALINE: Crushed caramelized nuts makes a delightful add-in because the cream softens the caramel just enough to take away the brittleness while still keeping the crunch. Follow the recipe for candied nuts on page 144, and layer them with the ice cream as it is packed for the freezer.

WHITE CHOCOLATE–HAZELNUT: If you are a fan of white chocolate, you'll find that the hazelnut is a great match. Use the hazelnut paste variation above and substitute white chocolate for the milk chocolate.

sorbets

Tomato-Cucumber (page 92)

TOMATO-STRAWBERRY: These two fruits are remarkably well-balanced. Omit the cucumbers and cilantro. Instead, sauté 2 pints of washed and hulled strawberries with the sugar, plus an additional 2 tablespoons, until juicy. Proceed with the directions, and serve this delightful concoction with a tiny drizzle of the very best, oldest, thickest balsamic vinegar you can afford.

Quince (page 96)

SPICED QUINCE: Quince poaching liquid can take any number of aromatic additions. Try a few chunks of fresh ginger, some star anise, crushed cardamom pods, or cinnamon sticks.

ROSEMARY-QUINCE: Like apples and pears, quince lends itself nicely to the pine-anise aroma of rosemary. Add ½ cup of crushed rosemary needles to the poaching liquid. After they are strained out their essence will linger.

ROSE-QUINCE: A splash of rose water in the blender will bring out the floral qualities of the quince. Don't overdo it, though; just ½ teaspoon should do the trick.

Mango (page 97)

MANGO, JAMÓN, AND OLIVE OIL: A hint of salt and savory is beautiful thing with a perfectly ripe mango. Replace the lime with lemon in this recipe, and just before freezing fold in 2 tablespoons of the best extra-virgin olive oil you have, and 1 cup of very finely diced or shredded jamón serrano, ibérico, Bayonne ham, or prosciutto. Really, any good, smoky ham will do. (But not that canned boiled stuff. Reserve that product for holding doors open.)

INDIAN MANGO: Much of the world thinks of the mango in terms of chutney. As it turns out, when you combine the traditional Indian flavors in a balanced way, it makes a killer sorbet. Add 3 to 4 crushed cardamom pods (or ½ teaspoon of ground cardamom), 1 inch of fresh ginger, and ½ cup chopped fresh cilantro leaves to the sugar and water boil. When the syrup has cooled, strain out these additives. Soak a mixture of golden raisins and dried currants in 1 tablespoon of sherry vinegar and hot water to cover, then set them aside to plump and cool. When cool, fold into the freezing sorbet, or sprinkle on top at serving time.

PINEAPPLE-MANGO: Add 1 cup of fresh diced pineapple to the blender with the mango and proceed with the recipe as directed. You can also try adding banana, guava, papaya, kiwi, dragon fruit, prickly pear, or really any tropical fruit. Get creative!

Poached Pear (page 98)

ORANGE-BAY POACH: Poach the pears in orange juice and a handful of crushed bay leaves. Serve it with some candied orange zest and a cider vinegar–caramel glaze.

WINE POACH: Cover the fruit with wine instead of water. Red or white both taste great, the red resulting in a wine-colored finished product. Add to the poaching liquid a cinnamon stick, 2 whole cloves, freshly grated nutmeg, star anise, a hunk of fresh ginger, and a slice of orange rind.

CIDER POACH: Follow the wine poach method, substituting apple cider for the wine. The effect will be similar, minus the wine's flavor, alcohol, and tannins.

CARAMEL POACH: Caramelize 2 cups of sugar to a dark amber color (see page 136). Remove from the heat and very carefully add 3 cups of water while whisking. (It is going to erupt like Vesuvius.) Bring the clear caramel water to a boil and use as poaching liquid for the pears. Add a tablespoon of crushed cardamom pods and a hunk of fresh ginger.

WHOLE POACHED PEARS: Poach some whole, peeled pears, too, and use them as a plate element. Be sure to simmer slowly when poaching whole pears. Too much bubble action can wreck the shape. For best results, simmer for 30 to 40 minutes, then remove from the heat, cool completely in the poaching liquid, and store in the liquid overnight. The color and flavor will penetrate deeply, and the finished fruit will be all the more flavorful. Use a half pear with the center core scooped away as a vessel for the sorbet. (Be sure to slice off a flat base so the pear doesn't rock), or hollow out the core and stuff it with cheese, chocolate, nuts, dried fruit, or all of the above.

Beet-Pistacho (page 102)

WATERCRESS-BEET: Omit the pistachios and add a cup of peppery watercress to the blender for a delightful palate cleanser.

HORSERADISH-BEET: This traditional pair takes on a new life when they're freezing cold. Omit the pistachios and add 1 tablespoon of prepared horseradish and a few twists of freshly cracked black pepper to the blender. Serve this as a savory starter with a Parmesan tuile, an onion and citrus salad, or floating in chilled borscht.

Carrot and Ginger (page 104)

CARROT-CORIANDER: A lovely combination that can go one of two ways. Add 1 tablespoon of coriander seed, toasted and crushed, to the hot simple syrup. Strain out the seeds from the cooled syrup before adding it to the blender. Or, you can add fresh green coriander, otherwise known as cilantro or Chinese parsley. Chop ½ cup of the fresh green leaves (no stems, please!) and add it to the puree as it goes into the freezer. Serve them as palate cleansers, appetizers (try tiny scoops on salted parsnip chips), or as a dessert, with coconut whipped cream, chocolate-dipped dried apricots, or orange-caramel sauce.

CARROT, CARDAMOM, AND HONEY: My favorite spice strikes again, adding a decidedly Indian flair to this recipe. Replace half the sugar in the simple syrup with honey, and add 3 to 5 crushed cardamom pods to the hot simple syrup. Strain them out of the cooled syrup before adding it to the blender.

CARROT, SAFFRON, AND NUTMEG: This trio is a delightful mix of sweet and savory. Toast 3 to 4 strands of saffron in a dry skillet for 30 to 60 seconds until crispy. Crush them and add them to the hot simple syrup, along with ½ teaspoon of freshly grated nutmeg. Then proceed with the recipe as directed, and serve with gingersnaps, or over a thick, warm slice of banana bread.

CARROTS AND RAISINS: This sorbet is just like your grandmother's old-fashioned carrot salad, only classier. Combine ½ cup each of raisins, golden raisins, and dried currants, add 1 tablespoon of apple cider vinegar, then cover with ginger ale or apple juice. Microwave for 30 to 60 seconds until hot, then set aside to plump and cool completely. Add to the base in the freezer, reserving a few to sprinkle on top at service. Serve with caramel-vinegar sauce (pages 136–37), peanut butter cookies, or candied walnuts.

Melon (page 106)

GELO DI MELONE: This Sicilian specialty is usually made in pudding form. But there is no reason we can't adapt it for the freezer! Make the recipe above with watermelon, and add to it ¼ of a vanilla bean, scraped. Proceed with the recipe as directed, then serve in the Sicilian manner, topped with whipped cream, chopped pistachios, chopped candied citron or lemon zest, grated chocolate, and a dusting of cinnamon.

HONEY-MINT MELON: Orange and green melons pair nicely with honey and mint. Replace the sugar in the above recipe with honey, and add ½ cup of finely chopped fresh spearmint leaves. You can leave the green bits in, or strain them out when the syrup has cooled.

GINGER-PEPPER MELON: Use very sweet orange or green melons. Add 2 tablespoons of crushed pink peppercorns and 1 tablespoon of freshly grated peeled fresh ginger root to the syrup, and proceed with the recipe as directed.

WATERMELON-ROSE: Make the above recipe using watermelon, and add 1 tablespoon of rose water to the syrup. Serve with a diced mixed melon salad dressed lightly in honey with a chiffonade of rose petals.

SPICY MELON AND CUCUMBER: Fruits doused in chile and lime are a common snack to be bought on the street corners of Los Angeles. Combine sweet melons and cucumber in the above recipe, add 1 teaspoon of New Mexico chile powder and an additional ¼ teaspoon of salt to the simple syrup. Serve over a chilled fruit compote of diced melon, mango, cucumber, pineapple, and jicama dressed with lime juice.

LI HING MUI–MELON: This Chinese condiment of tangy dried salted plums was made popular in Hawaii in the early 1900s. It comes in a powdered form, which is delicious sprinkled over sweet icy, fruity desserts. Try it here, dusted lightly over sweet melon sorbet.

sherbets

Fat-free Chocolate (page 110)

FULL-FAT CHOCOLATE: If you are not concerned about fat content, there are a couple options for a chocolate sherbet. You can use whole milk in the master recipe, or you can use whole milk and melted chocolate bars. Melt 6 ounces of dark bittersweet chocolate in the microwave for 30 to 60 seconds, stirring every 15 to 20 seconds so it doesn't burn. Slowly drizzle the sweet milk into the melted chocolate in the same manner described in the master recipe. Then, when it's finished, feel free to finish your presentation with some more decadent toppings. Try this method with milk or white chocolate, too.

PEANUT-CHOCOLATE: Again, there is fat in peanut butter, but yum! Stir 2 tablespoons of creamy peanut butter into the milk syrup until it is dissolved, then proceed with the recipe as directed. Be sure to serve with peanut brittle.

Blood Orange (page 111)

BLOOD ORANGE–BAY: Bay leaves and citrus are great friends. Add 3 to 4 pulverized bay leaves and ¼ of a scraped vanilla bean to the sugar and orange juice, and warm it all together. Then proceed with the recipe as directed.

BLOOD ORANGE–ANISE: Steep 3 to 4 star anise with the sugar and juice. Similar effects can be achieved with toasted and ground anise or fennel seeds. Serve with a shot of anise liqueur.

BLOOD ORANGE–CHILE: I won a culinary contest with this combination. It was the 1980s and the idea was unusual at the time. Add 1 tablespoon of red chile flakes to the sugar and juice and warm them all together. You can strain out the chile flakes before freezing if you like.

Agave-Lime (page 112)

PINEAPPLE-AGAVE: Omit the orange flower water from the above recipe. Before freezing, puree 2 cups of fresh pineapple in a blender, then add the master recipe base slowly to facilitate blending. Pass through a strainer to remove excess fibers, and freeze as directed.

Lavender-Almond (page 114)

LAVENDER-PEAR: Peel, core, and cut 3 ripe pears into chunks. Cover with water and boil until tender, then strain and set aside to cool. Place the pears in a blender and puree. Add slowly to facilitate blending, then freeze as directed.

BLUEBERRY, HONEY, AND LAVENDER: Combine a pint of fresh ripe blueberries with 2 tablespoons of honey in a small sauté pan over high heat and cook, stirring, until they get juicy and jammy. Cool completely, then add to the recipe. Pass through a fine-mesh strainer before freezing as directed. The berries give the dish a nice lavender hue.

LAVENDER-TANGERINE: Replace the almond milk with 2 cups of cow's milk. Warm the sugar, milk, lavender, and vanilla, then allow to cool completely. Strain and add 1 cup of tangerine juice and the zest of 2 tangerines before freezing as directed. You can do this with oranges, but the tangerine flavor is more floral and therefore more special.

Passion Fruit, Ginger, and Carrot (page 115)

PASSION FRUIT–YOGURT: Replace the milk with an equal amount of nonfat plain yogurt for a zingy variation.

PURE PASSION: For a straight passion fruit sherbet, omit the ginger and replace the carrot juice and 2 cups of milk with 3 total cups of whole milk. Heat the milk with the sugar and zest, then set aside to cool. Combine this liquid with 3 passion fruits, season with lime juice and salt, then proceed with the freezing as directed.

COCONUT–PASSION FRUIT: Omit the ginger, and replace the milk and carrot juice with a can of unsweetened coconut milk. If you do not have quite 3 cups of coconut milk, make up the difference with regular milk.

PINEAPPLE–PASSION FRUIT: Follow the Pure Passion variation above. Puree 2 cups of pineapple in a blender until smooth, then add the cooled passion fruit sorbet base. Pass it through a strainer before freezing as directed.

Persimmon (page 116)

PERSIMMON-GINGER-CORIANDER: Omit the tea bag and add 1 tablespoon of toasted coriander seed and 2 tablespoons of grated fresh ginger to the sweet milk, then proceed with the recipe as directed.

PERSIMMON-BACON: The smoky salty flavors of bacon work wonderfully with sweet persimmon. Add ½ cup crumbled crispy cooled bacon to the mix as it is being frozen.

TARRAGON-PEPPER-PERSIMMON: Omit the tea and replace it with ½ cup of chopped fresh tarragon leaves and ½ teaspoon freshly cracked black pepper.

WINTER SPICE–PERSIMMON: For this autumnal version, start by substituting brown sugar for the white sugar. Omit the tea bag and add 1 crushed cinnamon stick, ½ teaspoon grated nutmeg, allspice, ginger, and a tiny pinch of clove to the swect milk. Serve with whipped cream and Winter Fruit Compote (page 142) or sautéed caramelized persimmons.

Thai Iced Tea (page 118)

BUBBLE TEA SHERBET: Fat, chewy tapioca balls are added to create boba, or bubble tea. This fat-strawed sensation originated in Taiwan and spread throughout Southeast Asia before becoming extremely popular in the United States. You can find large tapioca pearls in any Asian market, or get them on-line. Some larger supermarkets carry smaller tapioca pearls in the baking aisle. They come in many colors, but have a neutral flavor. Cook ¼ cup of tapioca pearls in 2 cups of water. Boil, reduce the heat, and simmer for 15 minutes. Remove from the heat, cover, and set aside to cool and plump. Proceed with the recipe, and add cooled, softened tapioca to the recipe during the freezing process.

ORANGE-THAI TEA: Add the finely grated zest and juice of 2 oranges and 1 teaspoon of orange flower water after the milk mixture has cooled, and proceed with freezing as directed in the main recipe.

COCONUT-THAI TEA: Replace the milk with an equal amount of canned unsweetened coconut milk.

Indian Rose Water (page 120)

COCONUT-ROSE: Replace the milk of the recipe with canned unsweetened coconut milk. Talk about exotic!

granita

Classic Sicilian Granita (page 123)

MULLED AND SPICED: Adjust existing liquids to your specification by warming them with spice-and-herb mixtures, then allow to steep and cool. Try mulled wine, spiced apple cider, spiced cranberry juice, Turkish coffee, or chai tea.

Putting your personal stamp on a recipe is the best part of cooking. Cranberry-Pomegranate Sorbet is a warm-weather idea with an autumnal twist. Cook the berries with pomegranate juice until tender, then puree. Freeze with a handful of pomegranate seeds.

sugar 101

~~~~~

For novices, there are a few things it pays to know about cooking sugar. When sugar is liquefied by heat and cooked, it moves through several stages of thickness. They have names that correspond to their appearance, and the names also correspond to a temperature.

sugar table

TEMPERATURE °F	SUGAR STAGE	ICE TEST
212°F	Boiling	Forms a liquid thread that will not ball up
230–235°F	Thread	Can barely be formed into a ball
240–245°F	Soft Ball	Forms a soft, malleable ball
245–255°F	Firm Ball	Forms a ball that will flatten when squeezed
260–265°F	Hard Ball	Forms a ball that is difficult to manipulate
270–275 °F	Soft Crack	Firm threads form that will bend
275–280°F	Crack	Firm threads that will snap (crack) when bent, but may stick in teeth when eaten

TEMPERATURE °F	SUGAR STAGE	ICE TEST
285–315°F	Hard Crack	Firm threads that will snap (crack) when bent, and dissolve in teeth when bitten
325°F	Light Caramel	Firm crack with light golden color progressing to darker and darker color until it is carbonized
345°F	Amber Caramel	
350°F	Dark Caramel	
375°F	Very Dark Caramel	
400°F	Burnt Caramel!	

When cooking sugar, a candy thermometer is helpful, although they are not always reliable. I was taught to test the sugar by feel, which never ever fails.

When the spoonful of test sugar is drizzled into ice water, you will instantly be able to touch it, and manipulate it to judge its stage. If you can't form a ball with it, it is still in thread stage. If the ball is soft, it is soft-ball stage. If it is hard to form a ball, it is hard-ball stage. If, when you drizzle it on the ice it immediately solidifies and will crack easily, it is at crack stage. The difference between soft-crack and hard-crack can be best judged in your mouth. If the sugar sticks in your teeth, it's soft-crack. If it shatters and dissolves easily on the tongue, it is hard-crack. Hard-crack is usually very close to caramel, depending on any other ingredients that might be added, as happens in candy making. That means it is in the last stage before carbonization (aka burning; you don't want to get there).

When the sugar reaches the stage you want, you need to immediately remove it from the heat and use it. Sugar will continue to cook in the hot pot, and can easily increase in stage while sitting on the counter. (In the case of caramel, that means it can burn even off the heat and sitting on your counter.) In the case of Italian meringue, immediate use means pouring it directly into whipping egg whites that have already been beaten to a soft-firm peak.

One final note about cooking sugar—the easiest way to clean up a sugar pot is to boil it. Fill the sugar pot (even one that has crystallized) with water and bring it to a boil. The sugar will dissolve, and can be poured right down the drain. Why scrub hard when you don't have to?

CRYSTALLIZATION

One of the reasons cooks resist candy making and sugar cooking is the fear of crystallization. This is one of the few occurrences in cooking that has no fix. Once sugar has crystallized, the recipe is ruined and you'll need to start over. While it is a pain in the butt to start over, sugar is relatively cheap. That is why I encourage cooks to give sugar cooking a try. You will never really understand sugar cooking until you make mistakes.

glossary

ADD-INS
Garnishes folded into an ice cream, dough, or batter, such as chocolate chips, nuts, or raisins.

AMARETTO
An Italian liqueur with the distinctive flavor of bitter almonds.

ANISE
An annual flowering herb, related to parsley. The seeds have a distinctive licorice flavor, which is used in liqueurs, candies, sauces, and cosmetics.

BAIN-MARIE
Cooking with indirect heat, either hot water (see *water bath*), or steam (see *double boiler*).

BLANCH
To boil briefly, then submerge in ice water to halt the cooking. The process is used to loosen the skin and intensify the color of vegetables and fruits. Also referred to as *parboiling.*

BLOOM
1. The absorption of water by powdered gelatin.
2. The dusty film that appears on the surface of chocolate if it has gotten too cold (sugar bloom), or too hot (fat bloom).

BOBA
Fat, chewy tapioca pearls, or bubble tea, which contains boba.

CAJETA
A Mexican caramel sauce made from goat milk, available as a sauce in bottles and cans, or as a prepared candy.

CANDIED GINGER
Fresh-peeled ginger root, cooked in sugar syrup, and coated in sugar.

CARAMELIZED
To cook food until the sugar, naturally occurring or added, darkens to an amber "caramel" color. Caramelization brings out the food's deep, sweet, rich flavors.

CHIFFONADE
A leaf cut into thin, ribbon-like strips. It is achieved by stacking several leaves, rolling them like a cigar, and slicing off "coins" from one end of the cigar to the other. The technique is used frequently for basil and mint.

CITRON
A large citrus fruit used mainly for its thick, fragrant peel.

COGNAC
A fine, double-distilled brandy from the town Cognac and its surrounding region on the southwest coast of France.

CONFECTIONERS' SUGAR
Another name for powdered sugar. Also called *icing sugar.*

CREAMING
Blending two ingredients into a creamy, smooth, pastelike texture.

CURRANTS

Tiny raisins made from the miniature Zante grape. Do not confuse them with red, white, or black currants, which are small berries used for preserves, pastries, and the liqueur *cassis*.

DOUBLE BOILER

Two pots fitted one on top of the other, designed to allow steam from the bottom pot to rise up and warm the ingredients in the top pot. It is used when direct heat is too severe. Also known as a *bain-marie*.

FILBERTS

Another name for hazelnuts.

FOAM

Anything with air whipped into it, usually eggs, egg yolks, or egg whites. May also refer to whipped cream.

FOLDING

The gentle incorporation of two ingredients, usually one of which is a foam.

FUJI

A crisp, sweet Japanese apple variety introduced in the 1960s, popularized in the United States in the 1980s.

GANACHE

A pastry kitchen staple ingredient, made from equal parts cream and chocolate, used for fillings, truffles, glazes, and icings.

GRAND MARNIER

A French liqueur made from a blend of cognac and oranges.

HARD-CRACK STAGE

Sugar cooked to between 300°F and 310°F, used in candy and pastry making. When cooled, the sugar will harden and snap or crack easily.

ICE BATH

Ice water used to quickly cool foods. Foods can be placed directly in the bath, or set on top in another bowl, and stirred until cool.

ICING SUGAR

See *confectioners' sugar*.

KIRSCHWASSER (KIRSCH)

Cherry brandy, originally distilled in Bavaria from Morello cherries and their pits.

LI HING MUI

A Chinese condiment made from dried, salted, preserved plums, eaten whole or pulverized to a powder and sprinkled over fruits and desserts.

MACERATE

To soak food, usually fruit, in liquid to infuse flavor.

MICROPLANE

A fine grater used for citrus zest and hard cheeses. The tool was originally a carpenter's rasp used for sanding wood.

NIBS

Cocoa beans that have been roasted, hulled, and crushed. Used as an add-in for chocolate confections, they are only a couple of steps away from being chocolate. You can make chocolate by processing the nibs into a paste and adding sugar.

NUTELLA

An Italian trademarked product made from ground hazelnuts and milk chocolate. The product was first developed in World War II as a way to extend rationed chocolate.

PARBOILING

See *blanch*.

PARCHMENT PAPER

Heavy paper that withstands heat, water, and grease, used to line pans and wrap foods.

PÂTE À CHOUX

A pastry dough, known best for its use for making cream puffs, profiteroles, and éclairs.

PEAK

The stage at which a foam has been beaten so that it is thick and stiff. When the whisk is pulled out, the foam should form into a peak, or point.

REDUCE

To cook the liquid out of a dish, reducing its volume, intensifying its flavor, and thickening its consistency.

RIBBON

The stage at which an egg yolk–based mixture has been beaten so that it is thick and lighter in color. The term refers to the look of the mixture as it is scooped up and drizzled back down onto itself—when ready, "ribbons" should appear on the surface for a moment before sinking back into the mixture.

SAUTÉ

To cook food quickly, over high heat, constantly stirring for even browning. The term is French, and it means "to jump." Sauté pans are designed with a curved lip, making constant motion as easy as a flick of the wrist.

SEIZE

The thickening and hardening of melted chocolate that occurs when a small amount of moisture is added.

SIMPLE SYRUP

A pastry staple ingredient, made by boiling equal parts sugar and water. Used for moistening cakes, sweetening sauces and fruit purees, and as a recipe ingredient in sorbet.

SOFT-BALL STAGE

Sugar cooked to between 234°F and 240°F, used in candy and pastry making. When cooled, the sugar can be formed into a soft ball.

SOFT-CRACK STAGE

Sugar cooked to between 270°F and 290°F, used in candy and pastry making. When cooled, the sugar is hard, but still bends.

SRIRACHA

A Vietnamese sauce made from hot chiles, garlic, vinegar, and salt. It is often referred to as "rooster sauce," a reference to the rooster on the label of the best-selling brand, Huy Fong.

STONE FRUIT

A tree fruit that contains a pit, or stone, such as peaches, apricots, cherries, and plums.

SUPRÊMES

1. A section of citrus fruit that has been removed from its membrane. To get at the zest, cut the top and bottom off the fruit, cut all the skin off so that no white pith is visible (so the fruit looks naked), then slice out each section with a sharp knife.

2. Suprême also refers to the tender piece of chicken attached to the breast, sometimes called the "tender."

TEMPER

1. A process used to combine two ingredients of different temperatures, one of which is usually eggs, so that the shock of the temperature change does not affect the end product. A small amount of the hot ingredient is stirred into the cold eggs before the eggs are added, to ease the shock and prevent scrambling.

2. The process of manipulating the temperature of melted chocolate in order to align its molecules in a way that keeps the hardened chocolate shiny and crisp.

3. Bringing something frozen to a workable temperature, usually by letting it warm up at room temperature or in the refrigerator.

WATER BATH

A method in which a pan of food is cooked resting in another, larger pan of water (as in a baked custard). The method slows the conduction of heat, cooking slowly and gently. Also known in French as a *bain-marie*.

ZEST

The colorful outermost rind of a citrus fruit, containing high concentration of the essential oils and flavor compounds that flavor the fruit itself. The best way to access this is with a *microplane*.

index